# THE OTHER SIDE
# OF ADDICTION

## FROM TERRIFIED
## TO TRIUMPHANT

LAKITA GORDON

*The Other Side of Addiction*
Copyright © 2014 by LaKita Gordon. All rights reserved.

Scripture quotations marked (kjv) are taken from the *Holy Bible, King James Version, Cambridge,* 1769. Used by permission. All rights reserved.

This book is designed to provide accurate and authoritative information with regard to the subject matter covered. This information is given with the understanding that the author is not engaged in rendering legal, professional advice. Since the details of your situation are fact dependent, you should additionally seek the services of a competent professional.

Published in the United States of America

Cover designed by Rob Williams (Fiverr: Cal5086)
Interior layout by Katherine Watkins (Fiverr: iamgigpower)

ISBN: 978-0-69217-438-8
Biography & Autobiography /
Personal Memoirs

This book is dedicated to my grandmothers, Rosie E. Adams and Earline Tillman. Both of you told me that one day I would do something great. I love you both with an eternal love.

# ACKNOWLEDGMENTS

I would like to thank my personal Lord and Savior Jesus, the Anointed One, for chasing after me, keeping me, saving me, and protecting me even when I didn't know that he was.

To my mommy, Elizabeth A. Adams-Smith, you are strong, beautiful, funny and out-going. You have taught me some of life's greatest lessons.

To my daddy, John W. Dreher, for allowing me to see that Jesus performs miracles every day, for defeating addiction and being the best dad that you knew how to be.

To my twin sister, NaKita S. Woods (my little Weet Feet), and my bro in-law Kevin J. Woods Sr. (Bird), thank you for always being there and being a great example. We have been through many trials together and have overcome and are now able to teach our children how to be educated and respectful people who will contribute positively to society. We've had and always will have a bond that no one can break. I love you!

To my husband, Leroy R. Gordon, you are an amazing man, and beside the Lord, you have made me stronger and helped me to heal from past hurt and low self-esteem, and you have loved me just as Christ loves the church. You continue to render the affection that is due to me, and I'm thankful that you found your good thing (me).

My daughter, LaNaja Y. Gordon (scoopeez), you are beautiful, funny, wise, and a joy to be around. God has scooped up everything good that he has created and he rolled it into a beautiful little girl and gave her to me. I love you mini-me!

To my nephews Kevin, Devin, Evin, and Caleb, I love you all, and I know you'll be men after God's own heart! Thank you to Aunt Chelle, Aunt Tam, Aunt Rusty, and Nana for taking very good care of us. Thank you to my extended family Darrell and

LaShell Ruger, James and Michelle Morgan, and Stephanie Clay for being there to encourage me even before the first words were ever written. Iron really does sharpen iron!

The Gray/McLean family, the Adams Family, Dave and Becky Williams, and Tommy and Torrina Hudson for being a great family and I love you all. Thank you to the Dreher family, especially my aunts Sherita, Lissa, and Wanda—we missed time while I was growing up, but we've more than made it up, and I absolutely love being around you all! Thank you to the McClain family, and the Glover family for teaching me, taking me in and feeding me. I love you! Thank you to the McNeil Family and to my in-laws: Leroy and Barbara Gordon, Elaine & Audrey Young, and Kenyan and Caleb Gordon.

To Bishop George and Pastor April Davis and Faith Christian Center Jacksonville, where would my family be without your family and staff ? I thank God that you all were obedient to God's call on your life because you have imparted so much time, wisdom, and laughter into my life, and I've grown so much since I stepped into your presence and congregation in April 2002.

To JR (my biscuits), Delonte (what's happenin' baby?), Davon (swoop) (RIP), and my baby girl, my pookie, Keishawnna, I love you all and am glad I have the opportunity to be your cousin. We've all been through some similar situations and have grown to be triumphant and grateful for life.

# FOREWORD

I thought that as you grew older, the memories that you had as a child slowly fade away. Whether good or bad, I can recall these times in my mind as if they happened just yesterday. Some memories can cause me to stare off into space and smile as I watch my grandmother, twin sister, and cousin sitting in the park, eating bologna sandwiches and corn chips, the ranch-flavored ones, and drinking a little Hug juice, the blue one. While others cause me to wish that I was never born. Often times I wonder what the purpose of trials and obstacles are.

I've wondered time and time again why children are born to parents who didn't plan to have them and then the children suffer and are deprived of a life that could've been so much better than the one that they were given. But I have learned that you recognize and conquer obstacles one at a time and that in all that I do, there are choices that I have to make. And as I write this truth, I continuously ask myself many questions, such as, why is this life full of problems? Why do we have to endure pain, affliction, broken hearts and promises? Why are obstacles always staring us in the face? Why does life hurt so bad? Why am I here?

# THE FOUNDATION

I can remember growing up and feeling as if I was a mistake. Both of my parents were suffering from drug addictions, and my twin sister and I felt as if we were left to figure it all out on our own, as if life wasn't overwhelming enough with learning new things in school, learning how to be a kid, and just learning what it meant to overcome an obstacle.

I was only five or six years old when I first noticed a change in my mother. She seemed as if she was walking in space, and she was talking funny too. Her eyes were very shiny, and they hadn't always looked that way. And for the life of me, I couldn't remember why she would go away for what seemed like forever, and she would stay away for quite a while. But sometimes that was nice because then she wasn't always yelling and cursing at us and telling us how much we got on her nerves. To create some balance, my mother was not absent for every moment of my childhood and she was not mean and ornery every second of every day that she was in the home with me. My goal is to shed some light on how my life was impacted from the other side of addiction.

When my daddy would come around, it was not a good time. My mother would say mean things to him and even tell us to say mean things as well. But no matter what happened, I just couldn't bring myself to say anything mean to my daddy. I adored him. Although I saw him take food from the table and dump it down the garbage disposal just because he and Mom were having an argument, I still didn't think that he could do any wrong. The fact of the matter is he did some wrong as well. I witnessed him saying negative things and cursing at my mother and also physically abusing her.

No matter how my day is going now, I often revert back to the same question: why do I remember all of this? My twin forced herself to forget so many of these crucial and traumatic experiences and the details that come along with them. I must admit that she had it a little rougher than I did. Going forward, I don't want to diminish the work that my twin has done or convey her thoughts or experiences through my story. She constantly got yelled at, hit, and belittled just because she looked like our father. At first I didn't think that was so bad because at least she looked like someone. When I would ask Mommy who I looked like, she would say, "Child, you don't look like nobody." And that really hurt because it made me feel like I didn't belong in the family.

Life on Ninth St. and Wahler Pl. in Washington, DC, was so much fun! I recall days where we would run around playing hide-and-go-seek and put on our purple-and-white skates, and all of the kids in the neighborhood would skate through the neighborhood. But it was even more fun to skate on the little playground right across the street at Draper Elementary School, where we attended school from prekindergarten through sixth grade.

We'd sometimes get glass jars or soda bottles and catch bees and black jacks as they land on the honeysuckle bushes in the front yard of the fenced school yard. And sometimes, we'd gather up a group of girls who wanted to jump double dutch, and we'd jump-rope for hours, well, that is until the street lights came on. And we had to do any homework before we were allowed outside to play. Running, screaming, yelling, and hollering "Tag, you're it" and "Uh-oh, I was already on base" were a true joy.

The Other Side o f Addiction

During the summer months, we also had the chance to swim right there on the street corner when some unknown adult would open up the fire hydrant and block the street off and all of the kids would defy their parents and run through the gushing water. I was strictly told, "I just pressed your hair, and you better not step in a drop of water." And in my mind, I wasn't being disobedient because I never stepped in the water. I ran through it! We sometimes went up the hill and got a sandwich bag full of candy from the lady who was known as "the candy lady."

We'd have the go-go bands like Rare Essence and Sugar bear and E.U. to come and give free concerts on the hill. The sweet sounds of drumsticks thumping on overturned buckets, pots, and congos were, as we called it back in the day, bumpin'. I smile when I think of all of the times that the ice cream truck came through the neighborhood playing that same old, corny music that we all heard and recognized three blocks away. We were in charge of buying cigarettes for the adults, and then we could use a dollar to buy Bomb Pops, Icees, Now and Laters, Jingles, Double Bubble, Candy Necklaces, and a host of other stuff that we made sweet comforts and were a normal part of our daily lives.

# THE GOOD TIMES

Those good times that I remember were few and far between. My twin sister and I were born on April 19, 1979, at Greater Southeast Community Hospital. Due to the lack of technology that the world possesses today, our parents had no earthly idea that there were two babies. We had heard stories on numerous occasions where my mother repeatedly told the doctor,, "I don't have two babies nowhere and if I do, then one of 'em ain't coming home with me." Now of course we know that the latter part of that wasn't true. Thankfully, she had a great support system that would play a major role in our lives.

I can remember when my twin and I were in prekindergarten at Draper Elementary School. We grew up in what was considered the projects in Southeast, Washington, DC, or what we commonly referred to as "the real Souf-eas." We experienced many fun times playing outside with neighborhood kids as we played tag, hide-and-go-seek, Simon Says, and Mother May I? The adults on the block would block the streets off and turn the music up, and it was party time on Ninth Street and Wahler Place.

My grandma was the best grandmother in the whole world. While my parents were out partying and living it up while also battling drug addictions, it was my grandma who made sure that we ate and were clothed and bathed. We'd wake up bright and early in the morning, and Grandma would fix us the biggest bowl of oatmeal with raisins and some toast before we rushed outside to play. Who would've thought that many years later, I would really dislike oatmeal? It doesn't taste nasty, but the pure fact that I ate so much of it growing up makes me want to throw up every time I think about it. But as I think back to that time, the thought of my grandma's bowl of oatmeal with raisins and some warm, buttery toast makes me smile because she knew what was healthy and what was right for us, especially in the winter. Winter in the North made for some cold days and since we walked to school, grandma would always say, "Yall need something to stick to your bones because it's cold out there."

My grandma was so very special to me. She always had so much compassion in her eyes and did her very best to make sure that we were fed, clothed, and housed. She would occasionally take us to work with her at Howard University and at Sears at Landover Mall. And for Easter, she would always be sure that we were wearing something that was lavender. Once again, not that lavender is an ugly color, but I don't want to see it ever again in my life. I can only safely assume that it was her favorite color because she always found something lavender to buy for us. Every holiday, especially Easter, we had to wear a fu-fu lavender dress. Dresses were not my favorite piece of clothing to wear and that was because I couldn't climb the trees or clothes line pole with a dress on, and who wanted to shoot a three pointer with a dress on? Certainly not me.

And in case you may not have known it by now, I wasn't the girly-girl twin. I was never really into the baby-doll hair combing and dressing up and blah blah blah. But I was the one who loved to run and climb on stuff and play basketball and football. I never confused the male and female role, but I didn't find dolls fun at all. My twin adored the things and I could never understand why. They didn't do anything, and their joints snapped and popped when you bent the arms and legs and they just never made any sense at all.

Although we lived in what was considered to be the projects or the hood, we didn't know that it was called the projects or the hood until later on in life, when other people made it seem like it was the poorest and most horrible place to live on earth. For us, it was the place where we lived and the place where at any given moment you could ride through the neighborhood and see bunches of people sitting on their front or back porches and benches and sometimes you'd hear a different type of loud music as you walked or rode past certain houses. There were days when the streets were busy early in the morning, and the kids were outside all day long unless they were on punishment. And that even meant that you had to do something really bad in order for your parent/guardian to force you to stay in the house. We took pride in our neighborhood and there was a great sense of camaraderie.

Another special treat for me was when I and Twin would be sure to get with Grandma and plant her favorite flowers along the side of the house. She absolutely loved tulips, and we used to spend a lot of time every year planting them with her. We had the best time with our grandma when it was time to plant those flowers, and it absolutely got on her nerves when people would cut through our yard and trample on them.

Everyone in the hood knew that if you trampled on Miss Edna's tulips, it was on! Her name was Rosie Edna Adams, and I didn't understand why her favorite flower wasn't a rose. Some people called her Miss Rose, and others referred to her as Miss Edna. We knew that people would continue to cut through the yard and mess us what little grass we had, but she wanted to plant the tulips anyway. And she fussed and fussed because people constantly cut through the yard, but there was never much grass to begin with, and I didn't understand what the big fuss was all about. Planting flowers was just one of the ways that we could spend time with the one person whom we felt wanted us around.

We also spent numerous hours at the dining-room table putting puzzles together, and when she could, Grandma would take us to Hains Point park and pack us some delicious cut- down-the-middle bologna-and-cheese sandwiches with some crispy, seasoned Frito-Lay corn chips and delicious little Hugs juices. It was definitely a sad time when my grandmother got sick and had a stroke or triple bypass surgery and had to take so many medications. I never understood how a person with such a good heart could suffer so many sicknesses and ailments. At this point in life I thought that as long as you did good deeds, then you shouldn't be sick or suffering from anything.

I'd have to say that putting puzzles together was my favorite time with her. It was quiet, and she gave us space to grow, develop, and even makes some mistakes. Even with putting the puzzles together, I'm sure that she knew that we would mess up some of the pieces, but she never screamed at us because of it. She allowed us to experiment and learn things. And then she'd teach us why what we did was wrong and that there were consequences for any behavior, whether it was good or bad. But it was a great experience, and the time that we spent with her was a blessing.

## *Life Lesson:*

Cherish any time that you have to spend with the ones that you love. And ask as many questions as you possibly can in order to get direction from experienced family members like your grandparents. Cherish the quiet times when you sit down and enjoy peace. Listen to the stories that your elders have to tell you, and learn what they went through so that you can live a successful and victorious life. Grandparents are valuable, and they have worked hard, struggled, and fought for our rights. We should do all that we can do to honor them!

# WHERE CHANGE BEGAN

"Y'all betta come on here! I don't have all day, and y'all betta' not get dirty."

Now one thing that I didn't understand is why we had to walk so far every day, and secondly, if you dress us up in these cute little sailor-skirt outfits that are predominantly white, how are we supposed to "not get dirty?" These things didn't make sense to a six-year-old, but I wasn't even close to being brave enough to communicate that to my mom. We'd always have to walk from Robinson Place to Ninth Street and Wahler Place, each and every day. I was so sure that when we grew older, we would have some very strong legs because of all of the walking that we did.

My daddy had a car, but he was hardly ever around, and we never knew exactly why he wasn't around. We just knew that every time that he was around, he and Mom would start arguing. They argued right in front of us, but we didn't understand what they were talking about. The arguments always seemed so petty, and my twin and I were somehow made the subject of the arguments. Whenever we went on one of our little walking sprees, Mom would walk so fast and would constantly turn back and yell at us because we didn't have legs long enough to keep up with her. We tried our hardest to keep up, and the walk was a long one. Sometimes we'd have to jog in order to keep up, and it started to make me feel bad when Mommy made it seem like it was our fault that we couldn't keep up with her. I was so happy on the days when my art teacher, Mrs. Nelson, would drive by and stop to give us a ride since she worked at the school that we were hiking to get to. It was a true relief when she'd ride by, and most mornings, I would look for her car.

Now it was a short time after this little "betta not get dirty" fiasco that Daddy had shown up while we were in the room playing. And when we heard his voice, we dropped whatever it was that we were holding, and it was left unattended and abandoned. Whatever we were doing never mattered when we heard Daddy's voice. Daddy was here, and nothing else mattered at that moment in time, and that's the way it always was.

"Daddy, Daddy, when did you get here?" We would always sing in unison because twins did that quite often. We were always so amazed at how we would say the same thing at the same time, but we didn't discuss it before we said it. Each time that we spoke as one, we'd look at each other and, in unison, again say, "Heeeeeeey, stop it!" It was a great laugh, and it never got old to us. We were so amazed that we were twins, and our bond was, and still is, unbreakable. We don't always agree, but we are so close and have always been able to maintain a close relationship.

Daddy scooped us up, one in each arm, and kissed each of our cheeks and said, "Hey, my babies, what are y'all doing?" We looked forward to the way that he greeted us. He would always scoop us up and squeeze us and kiss our cheeks. And even if he saw what we were doing, he always asked anyway. It seemed like that's all Mommy needed to hear, and she asked angrily, "Why you so concerned about what they doing 'cause your sorry self ain't never been concerned no other time?"

Now from my point of view all I could wonder was, what in the world could she be so mad about? I mean, he had done nothing more than walk through the door and pick up his two favorite little girls and hug and kiss us. "Twins, y'all go back in your room and play." For whatever reason, Mommy would always The Other Side of Addiction rip that happy moment away so quickly, and then the arguing would begin. We were only concerned with basking in our father's presence and enjoying him whenever we had the chance and that moment always lasted for that amount of time, a moment. So we sadly, but obediently, climbed down from our daddy's arms and slowly walked into the room with our heads down. The excitement that we had just a few minutes ago had been swiftly snatched away, and we could no longer enjoy our toys.

And of course, we couldn't express ourselves to adults because that would be considered talking back to an adult and it was never tolerated, so the only option that we had was to argue with each other. "You get on my nerves" and "Just shut up, and get out of my face" filled the air because we were so very frustrated and didn't know how to let it out. And I thought, *Maybe that's what was wrong with Mommy.* I mean, she always said these same words to us. Each time I heard them, I became more and more confused as to why we got on her nerves, what nerves were, or why she would leave and not come back when she said that she would. I constantly thought to myself, *What are we doing to make her act this way?* But what could I do?

After Daddy left in a hurry and the door slammed, Mommy was at the living room window, yelling and cussing at Daddy. And she told me and Twin to come to the window and repeat the very words that we'd get slapped in the mouth for repeating any other time. And I didn't know if I would get slapped for saying the bad words or if I would get slapped for not saying them. But either way, I'll just have to take the slap because I was not going to say any bad words to Mommy or Daddy because I love them and it just didn't seem like the right thing to do.

It was really confusing to hear Mommy tell us, "You do as I say and not as I do." When I was old enough to understand that phrase, it still didn't make any sense at all. How could you teach a person not to do something and then you did it constantly? I was extremely observant as a child and I watched people constantly, including my parents. I did it because I wanted to learn what to do and the correct way to do it, and I was thoroughly confused because I was told to do one thing and my parents did another. My mom would constantly say, "I betta not hear y'all cussing and acting like you don't have no home training," and whenever Daddy was around, he'd say, "Y'all share and don't fight each other because y'all are family."

I didn't want to cuss anyway because it was associated with anger, and I didn't like the screaming and yelling. It didn't feel good to be screamed or cussed at. And Twin and I had no problem sharing because we loved each other so much and we shared every ounce of space that there was. We learned early on that we were to stick together and it came natural to us. But I was also taught to mind my manners and to obey when I was told to do something and with no backtalk. In this particular situation, I felt as if I was going to get slapped either way, and since the instructions were coming from Mommy, I didn't know whether to repeat after her or not.

## *Life Lesson:*

Children are always watching what the people around them are doing. It is extremely important to not only tell your children to do the right thing, but to be a living example. It thoroughly confuses a child when you teach them one thing and then you live something different. Although you don't notice it when they are young, they slowly lose respect for you, and by the time they are teenagers and you try to correct the situation, then it's much harder. If you teach your children to do the right thing, then live what you teach!

# THE GLASS TUBE

After the fiasco with Mommy trying to make us cuss at Dad had ended, Mommy sent us back in the room to continue playing. But shortly after that, I heard about three or four other voices in the living room. It sounded like they were having a great time too. There was music and plenty of laughter, and I wanted to see what was going on. So, I figured I'd just do what the typical child would do. In my mind, I thought that no adult could figure out what a smart child like me could be up to. So I cracked the door just wide enough to separate the door from the door frame and whispered, "Ma, I have to use the bathroom."

Now I knew good and I knew well that she couldn't have heard my pathetic excuse for trying to escape the room. I enjoyed my room that I shared with my twin, and the only thing that I really didn't like was all of the dolls were strategically placed around the room. I mean, dolls were on the closet shelves, sitting and relaxing against the walls on the floors, and sometimes, when I opened up a dresser drawer, there was a doll just lying there. I was not happy about it, and it was downright spooky. But smart little me, now I had a reason to leave, and I convinced my twin to follow me on the world's greatest adventure.

I had the excuse of Mom not hearing me when I told her that I had to use the bathroom. I promised Twin that she could take her favorite little baby doll with her, and she hesitantly agreed.

"Kita, we gon' get a beatin' if we get caught, and we gon' get in trouble 'cause Ma told us to stay in this room." A lot of the time, my mom threatened to beat us, be she didn't. But as a child, you never know when it'll actually happen and my twin was always the more cautious one. She was not weak whatsoever, just way more cautious than I was.

I frustratingly replied, "You are suuuuuch a scaredy cat."

And she aggressively replied, "Shut up, I ain't scared of nothing." I knew that was not true because Twin was scared of everything. She was always so afraid of what might happen, what did happen, what happened in the past, and so on.

So we headed out of the room on our adventure. Our bedroom was right beside the living room where the party was, so we didn't have to walk very far. But to make it more adventurous, we slowly and lightly tiptoed toward the rear of the apartment alongside the wall and then back down the hall toward the living room. And I saw Ma and three other people around the coffee table, and they were bent over it as if there was something very interesting on it. So I crept forward and backtracked a few times just for effect until I reached the crowd that was hovering over the dining room table even more than they were when we first walked out of the room. And I noticed that something smelled funny. The smell was kind of like the smell that you get when you have a gas stove and you spill something on the burner and it sticks to the burner or side of the burner and it scorches.

Well, when I peeked through two of the people that were bent over the table, I saw a glass tube that looked burnt and smoke was coming from it. All that I could think about was the fact that someone could get hurt. Mommy told us not to play with fire or we might get burned. I immediately determined that this glass thing was of no importance or interest to me, so I quickly dismissed what I saw and disrupted the crowd and said, "Ma, I'm hungry." And she slowly backed away from the table with smoke rolling from her lips, and I was so scared because I thought that

Mommy's mouth was on fire or that she was licking a glass bottle that was on fire. But then it dawned on me that if she could speak and she's not running around screaming or crying, then she wasn't hurt.

"Girl, didn't I tell you to keep your butt in that room?"

Again, all I could do was sadly walk back to what I commonly referred to as the room of doom. It seems as though every time something got interesting, we had to stay in that room. Furthermore, I couldn't shake the scene that I had just seen. Why would four grown-ups be sitting around a burnt clear glass bottle with smoke coming out of it?

My little mind pondered and pondered over that sight for days. I just didn't understand what was so much fun about a glass bottle with smoke coming out of it. But maybe grown-up fun was much different than kid fun.

## *Life Lesson:*

Be mindful of who and what you expose your children to. Whether they be family or not, be mindful of who influences your child. We all have the freedom to do whatever we want within the four walls of our own home. But seeing my mom and others doing drugs is something that I should never have seen. I am now thirty- four years of age, and I still remember it as if it were today. Always be mindful that your children are watching you, and you should be mindful of what you allow them to see. Experiences and exposure like the one above can have a lasting impression on the heart and mind. This one particular incident was the start of an emotional battle and many sleepless nights.

# THE SLIP UP

One particular Saturday, we were playing in the room of doom while Mommy was still asleep. We had some blue Rainbow Brite cars that came with little dolls with them. Rainbow Brite had multicolored clothes on and multicolored pillows to match. The whole doll thing was just not my cup of tea, so I would always remove the doll and I thought up a new idea for her fly ride that she came with. It was an actual car, and it just so happened that it was big enough to fit our little feet in.

So we took turns, quietly, or what we thought was quiet, and we skated across the floor. Of course, the floors were hardwood, so it made it seem louder than it actually was. Knowing that this aggravated Mom, we tried to skate as quietly as possible because she was not a happy camper when she was awakened from her sleep. She was the type to have to get up on her own or no one was happy that day.

The list of things that aggravated Mommy was growing more and more. And we had gotten to the point that although we were young, we felt that we didn't make Mommy happy. It seemed like every time we asked a question or did just about anything, she would get upset about it and yell. If I recall correctly, her favorite line was, "Y'all are getting on my nerves."

We knew what the consequences were for skating across the floor, but it was so much fun that we couldn't help but to do it. And sometimes Mommy seemed to wake up angry even when we were quiet, so we figured that we might as well have some fun, anyway. She also seemed to sleep forever on the weekends. Now I know that kids can go to bed extremely late and still wake up extremely early, but Mommy was always tired, and she loved to sleep. Once she awakens from her extended slumber, she would bathe us and attempt to pick us out something to wear. Remembering that she had neglected to separate our seasonal wardrobe, she would frustratingly state, "I have got to do something with all of this summer crap."

It always surprised me that Mommy would cuss so much because she told us not to say those kinds of words. And before I knew it, my six-year-old twin replied quickly yet innocently by saying, "What summer crap?" Twin was always repeating stuff that she heard other people say. Well, Mommy used another word instead of crap, and Twin did the same. And not that she said this intentionally, but she used to repeat after me so much because it aggravated the goodness out of me, and it just eventually became second nature to her. Now this may not seem so exciting to some, but in my head all that I could picture was twin running in circles around the room trying to escape the belt hitting her bottom. Because I was the more outgoing and outspoken of the two, it felt so good not to be the one in trouble this time.

Well, I sat back with my eyes wide open and my mouth in the most perfect oval shape because I knew she was about to get the whoopin' of her little young life. Twin immediately burst into tears when she realized that she just said a cuss word. She began to beg and plead to Mommy and repeat, "I didn't mean iiiiit." But all Mommy could do was fall over and laugh until she cried. I cried and laughed too! But I'm not sure if I was crying because mommy was crying or because I was so disappointed that the whoopin' of the year wasn't actually going to happen.

Now this was just the most peculiar scene ever, beside the smoking glass bottle. I don't know how in the world Mommy was laughing so hard and the whoopin' never showed up. Then *ding!* My light bulb came on, and I thought, *Wow, we can cuss now and mommy will laugh about it.* It hadn't been long before this incident that Mommy was flat out telling us to cuss, but I never knew that cussing was so funny. Normally, when my parents were cussing at each other, their brows were furrowed and they never

ever laughed and especially to the point of crying. Nevertheless, I was still afraid to try it. But if I ever did, at least I knew what Mommy would do. Another thing that I didn't understand was how mommy could cuss so much, but people constantly said that those words were bad words. So if these words are so bad, then why do people say them all the time?

I sometimes hated when the weekend was over because it was back to walking for what seemed like a hundred miles just to get to school. I didn't understand why Daddy had a car but was never available to take us to school or pick us up and take us places. Whenever my mommy and daddy were together, they'd just scream and cuss about stuff that didn't even seem to be important. Of course, to a six-year-old like me, I didn't even know what *important* was.

Twin and I often thought that they argued so much because of us. We thought the same about Mommy. We thought that she never wanted us around since we "got on her nerves" so much. I just wanted to play and be happy, and I wanted my mommy and daddy to get along and not scream and hate each other, especially while we were right in front of them. It made me sad, and sometimes I even cried because I didn't want to see them that way, and there were two things that hurt the most—there was nothing that we could do about it and we had figured at an early age that they argued and cussed so much because of us.

But to see two people who are supposed to love each other screaming and cursing all the time was just sad and confusing to a child. I often wondered why two people who are so unhappy would even come around each other anyhow. At that time, I didn't know where babies came from, but if the two of them came together and conceived us, then why did they?

We played it off and continued to try and ignore the arguing, cussing, and screaming, and oftentimes we would just continue to play as if we hadn't heard a thing. But we did hear them and we did notice, and it saddened us. Twin and I were always able to ask each other questions that no one could answer, just to clear our little heads and try to make sense of all of the anger and hostility. We constantly asked each other, "Why did they have us? What did we do? Why don't they stop? Why don't they want us?"

## *Life Lesson:*

Never put your child/children in the middle of the parents' arguments. Children should never be forced to deal with adult issues. Neither should they feel guilty for being born. Adults should never expose their children to arguing, cussing, and screaming at each other. Disagreements should be handled among adults, and instead of inserting the children into the disagreement, its better to get to the root of the actual problem. Using your child/children as a weapon is never going to fix any problem that you have, nor will it be the best thing for your child/children.

# LATE NIGHT PRANK

A couple of weeks had gone by, and when Daddy came over it was a true joy to see him. Twin and I had been up all morning, having a good time with our toys. Well, Twin was having a good time with those disgusting little dolls while combing their hair and switching their clothes and blah blah blah.

You know, I don't know why I continued to get those funky little plastic girls just because Twin wanted them. I despised them and showed absolutely no interest in dressing them up and doing their hair, simply because "they're not real and they're not going anywhere." I mean, you spend half an hour combing through the tangled silky hair and putting on just the right color shoes to match their beautiful evening gowns for this big imaginary ballroom extravaganza that was never going to happen. And I was so not interested in any of that.

But Twin, on the other hand, seemed to get the greatest joy out of primping and prepping those plastic things for nothing. And every chance that I got, I made it my personal business to make it more eventful for her. For example, one night, she went to sleep and I was wide awake. She often got up in the middle of the night to use the bathroom, and since I knew that she did this quite often, I got up out of bed and fumbled quietly through the dark while trying not to wake her. Once I got my hands on a couple of the dolls, I quietly popped all of their heads and limbs off and strategically laid them out on the floor.

All that I could imagine at this moment was how brilliant I was because I was able to carry out this master plan of torture in the complete dark and how horrified twin would be when she saw my well-planned and executed masterpiece. Then I scooped up all of the limbs and heads placed them in a Lego bucket and quietly exited the room and went into the bathroom, closed the door, and turned the light on. I sat happily on the bathroom floor and mixed and matched all of the doll babies body parts and heads. Some of the white dolls had black arms and white legs, and some of the black dolls had their heads jammed into the hole where the arms were supposed to go. It was brilliant and hilarious!

Well, since I was in the bathroom in the middle of the night, I had to make it seem like I was really using the bathroom. So I flushed the toilet, and as it filled back up with water, I strategically placed the mismatched dolls in the toilet and let them float on their backs, and some floated facedown (for effect). We were taught to always wash our hands after using the bathroom. As I giggled with content, I turned the water on and quickly washed my hands and quietly exited the bathroom and into the short, dark hallway that led to our bedroom. I crawled back into bed and watched as my sister stirred occasionally. When she did finally get up and stumble to the bathroom, the sheer sound of horror that escaped her lips was extremely gratifying to me. I felt like I had accomplished what I had set out to accomplish. I ran into the bathroom and told her to hush her mouth as she stood crying and repeating, "Kita why you do that?" I simply told her that the dolls themselves did it and that I tried to stop them. I looked at her sympathetically and said, "At least you don't have to pee no more."

For some odd reason, and although I was only six years of age, I had started to have trouble sleeping. I had started to think on and replay certain things that I had seen. These things seemed to be weird to me, but I'm not even sure that I knew what the word *weird* meant, so for now we'll use the word different. For example, I just didn't understand why Mommy and Daddy would scream and cuss at each other when they started their visits off on such a happy note. And it didn't seem to bother them too much, so I didn't have the slightest idea as to why it kept me awake.

Some nights I'd lie down, and all I could hear when I closed my eyes were things like "You don't do nothin' for them" and

"'Cause you always thinking everything gotta go your way." Well, my dad stuttered and whenever he got excited, he'd stutter a little more than usual. Maybe it was me and Twin, but we could never figure out if we did anything. What we did know for sure was that Mom would start to yell at us at the end of their fight, throw something, or just leave.

One thing that was keeping me awake this particular night was what I referred to as the "happy glass." I still couldn't figure out why Mommy and her friends were bent over this glass tube thing with smoke coming out of it and they were so excited about it. I mean, it was simply a burnt lightbulb with a tube of smoke coming from it. Plus, it smelled funny. Well, maybe it was the smell that made them giggle so much.

I don't know why my young mind pondered over such things, but I couldn't help it, and I tried to close my eyes really tight to squeeze the images and arguments away, and the only thing that was accomplished by doing this was that now my eyes hurt from squeezing them so tightly.

# *Life Lesson:*

Exposing your children to certain things, especially at an early age can be traumatizing to them. You may not notice the effects right away, but it doesn't mean that there aren't any effects. Seeing my parents constantly arguing, physically fighting, screaming and cussing kept me awake for years. Being exposed to these things tormented my mind and was the beginning of me suffering from depression. All of the arguing and putting me and my twin in the middle of it made us feel as if we were the cause of their unhappiness and that neither of them wanted us to be born. Seeing my mom do drugs planted a seed of curiosity and since it seemed to make her so happy, it made me want to try it. Exposure at an early age can be crucial to a child as they grow up.

# DADDY COMES BACK

I didn't know how long it had been, but it surely seemed like some years had gone by before we saw Daddy again. And I just didn't understand it. I was tired of going to bed at night and then waking up day after day and my daddy hadn't called or stopped by. Of course, only about a week had actually passed, and at this point in time, I didn't even care if they argued or fussed. I just wanted to see my daddy. But there was nothing that I could do about that.

I couldn't wait to wake up in the morning so that I could go to school. There were so many fun things at school. But before that could happen, Mommy had to find a way for Twin to stop crying. Every single morning, she would wake up and sit in the middle of the bed and just cry. And every single morning, Mommy would say, "What are you crying for?" and I wondered why she would ask the exact same question every day. She got the exact same answer every single time, and that was, "I dunno." I almost thought that it was a game that they enjoyed playing. It wasn't very funny to me, and in fact, it was downright aggravating. I got tired of waking up to her slow, steady crying every morning. And she dragged it out for what seemed like an hour. Even when Mommy would leave out of the room, I would whisper angrily to her, "What do you keep crying for?" I thought that she would certainly tell me, but all that me or mommy ever got was "I dunno."

Each morning that we awoke, we had the exact same routine. We had to get our teeth brushed, our faces washed, and then we marched over to our clothes, which were labeled with our names on the tags because we wore the same size. Mommy even wrote our names on our days-of-the-week panties. I thought that days-of-the-week panties were the best thing ever. I mean, I never had to guess or get confused about what day it was because some genius was brilliant enough to put it on our underwear. I was so excited about my panties. As you can see, I've always been a person who likes things in order, and I was never into working harder, but being smarter.

It was so very cool to have a twin because I always had someone to play with and pick on, and she was so easy to boss around. I know it's pretty corny, but the fact that I was a whopping eleven minutes older meant a lot in our world. I was technically older, and she could never dispute that.

Another week or more had gone by and still no sign of Daddy. That was, until one Saturday morning when we woke up early in the morning to play and make our usual noise. I heard Daddy standing outside of the window calling for Mommy to open the door. See, where we're from it was a rather normal thing to stand outside of an apartment building at any given time of the day or night and just yell for the person that you wanted to see. It was common and plenty of people had done it, and it didn't bother anyone around them. So Mommy got up and opened the door, and of course, Daddy's favorite little girls ran and jumped up in his arms before he could even get into the door good.

"Heeeey, babies, how y'all doin'?"

I was relieved, and I physically exhaled and said, "Aaaaah…" The sweet sound of my daddy's words just made me smile from ear to ear. And Mommy was in a good mood too because she was smiling and was happy. She got us dressed, and we went out for a ride in my daddy's car, a burgundy Cutlass. Twin and I really loved the Cutlass. Just the smell of Daddy's Brut aftershave and the familiar feel of the seats always made us super happy. It never mattered where we were going or who we were going to see, and as long as we were with our mommy and daddy, and they were not arguing and yelling, we were extremely happy.

We rode and rode around until Twin and I fell asleep in the backseat. When we finally did wake up, we were stopped on the hill. The Ninth Street and Wahler Place neighborhood was commonly referred to as "the hill." And it was so great that my grandma Rose lived directly across the street from our elementary school, on the Ninth St. side. And my godmother, whom everyone called Nana, lived on the Wahler Place side. It felt so good to have two grandmothers that I absolutely loved in my life.

I enjoyed being around my grandma Rose and my Nana at any time of the day and on any day of the year. I enjoyed my mommy too, and whenever we asked her for something and she said no to something, then Nana and Grandma would make it happen anyhow because that's just what grandparents did. As soon as Mommy would turn her back, they'd always give us whatever we wanted.

## *Life Lesson:*

Try and provide a happy environment for your children to grow up in because most times, what they see most is what they will do. Parents are so fixated on their children telling the truth no matter what, being respectful and courteous, and to do the right thing no matter what. And one crucial part that parents often forget to do: they forget to be the example. Always lead by example. Children don't need to be bought, and what matters most is that they want a happy environment and some good quality time. A positive environment sets a child up to be self-confident and have a positive self-image. It makes a child feel as if they can become anything that they want to and it helps them to cope with issues that arise outside of the home. Create a positive environment for your children because it makes a big difference!

# GETTING PHYSICAL

We awoke to arguing and cussing as we squirmed in the backseat of the Cutlass, and that always freaked me out. And I know that if I was scared, then Twin was certainly scared. After all, Twin was scared of everything! All I could think about was, *Why in the world were they arguing now?* All of these nice moments always turned into battling matches, and it was starting to really make me sad.

They stood on the side of the street and just went back and forth with these mean things that they said to one another. We always got kicked out the room when grown-ups were having fun or when they were arguing with each other. And I sure wish they would kick us out right now because that arguing drove me up a wall. And we didn't even know what they were screaming about, but our names would always be in the midst of the arguments. Mommy was always yelling, "You don't do nothin' for my kids," and Daddy was always replying with, "Ay...ay...ay...when I try to do stuff for my babies, you always got somethin' to say." No it's not a typo—Daddy stuttered quite a bit when he got excited. And Mommy seemed to know exactly what to say or do to get him to stuttering.

The next thing we knew, Daddy was grabbing mommy and pushing her up against the car. We didn't know whether to scream or run across the street to get help or what. Mommy struggled to get free, and all she kept saying was, "Get off of me, you betta get your hands off of me." And right on cue, Twin did what she did so very well—she began to cry. And I wanted to cry too, but someone had to calm Twin down and protect her because Mommy and Daddy weren't doing a very good job. I thought that strangers were the ones that argued and fought with one another. I didn't know that parents did it too.

People who were driving by took the time to stop and try to get Daddy off of Mommy. Back in the day, people intervened and tried to protect other people. But society today has people just "minding their own business." Back in the '80s, people knew who their neighbors were and even the one who lived down the street. People could also correct other people's kids, and it was okay. Children feared the teachers because the teachers had permission to spank a child who had gotten out of hand.

I wonder if all my friends had a mommy and daddy that screamed and yelled and argued and cussed like mine did. With me being the braver of the two of us, I pushed twin behind me and walked up and tried to break my parents apart, but to no avail. I walked quickly toward the two of them, who were at this point tangled up together, and I can remember trembling and wanting to just break down and cry because of how scared I was. But somebody had to stop this before it ended even worse than it was going now. So I finally yelled, "Just stop it...stop it. Get off of my mommy." No woman deserves to be beat on and no matter if my mom had issues or not, I didn't want anyone to hurt her. There were times that she was around and she was not absent all of the time. From a child's perspective, it was a lot because there are critical times where we needed her. Mommy was truly a sweet, funny and nice woman who enjoyed being around people. She was always sociable and considerate when she wasn't high. I didn't want to get a whoopin' for yelling at daddy, but he was hurting my mommy. Plus Mommy yelled at him whenever he was around, and that normally made him stop whatever he was doing and just leave, not to be seen for days or weeks. And thankfully that worked.

We didn't know if we should run and hug Mommy or Daddy, so we just stood there in utter amazement and great relief at the same time. Then Mommy snatched us by the arms as if we were the ones that had just pushed her around. That was one of the scariest events that I had witnessed in my little life at that point. Mommy crossed the street and yelled, "You betta hope one of my brothers ain't in this house."

And when we did get to Grandma's house, she had already heard the commotion outside, and she proceeded back inside for what seemed like a split second. My grandma was considered to be gangsta and was Madea way before Tyler Perry was. She came storming out of the house with her robe, or moo moo on, and walked toward Daddy so quick that I really thought that would be the last time that we saw him. She had a gun in her right hand and a glass of something in her left. I was amazed because she was going to shoot with one hand and then take a swig of whatever with the other hand. I adored Grandma and didn't want her to hurt daddy, but all I could think about was that Grandma was gangsta!

We needed to be consoled as well, but who was there to do it? In the midst of it all, nobody ever checked on us and asked us if we were okay. Everyone talked about the incident for a while and returned to their normal routines.

## *Life Lesson:*

Never force a child to choose between their mother and father. It is not good for children to be put in a position to have to choose between the two people who came together and conceived them. There should be no verbal or physical abuse in front of the children because what that does is teach the child that abuse is normal, and they will accept it from their mate/spouse when they get older. Whether your children are male or female, they should have a male and female example of what to look for in a spouse.

Fathers should be speaking to their daughters with respect and letting them know how beautiful they are, opening doors for them, and making them feel as if they are the most beautiful girl in the world. Fathers should be teaching their sons how to be good men. They should be teaching their sons what chivalry is and how they are to treat women with respect and not abuse them. Mothers should be nurturing and loving yet bringing correction when it's needed. Mothers should teach their daughters how to dress appropriately, take care of their personal hygiene and how to be a virtuous woman.

It's the small things that count with children, and teaching them these life lessons prepares them for life and equips them to be assets in society.

# A SCARY WALK HOME

By this point in my little life, things seemed to be getting rougher and more difficult for me to understand. At times, Mommy acted a little weird, and Daddy just didn't come around as much. Well, to say that he didn't come around as much is an understatement because he hardly ever came around. Maybe it's because of that time that I yelled at him to get off Mommy when he was shaking her and hitting her. And that made perfect sense to a seven-year old like me because when Mommy would yell and cuss at him, he'd disappear for a long time too. But I didn't even cuss.

I had planned to apologize to Daddy when I saw him again, whenever that might have been, because I didn't mean it. I just didn't know what else to do. This made me terribly sad, and I spent so much time crying at night when everyone else was asleep. After all, I didn't sleep as well as Mommy and Twin. I mean, how could I rest when all of this stuff kept happening back to back? So there I lay crying until I couldn't cry anymore. And another thing that I didn't understand was how this wasn't affecting anyone else. Well, I know it affected Twin, and I guess we just cried at different times. Whenever she was crying, I couldn't because she needed someone to help her to stop crying, and Mommy would probably get mad if both of us were crying at the same time.

Sometimes we'd be in the room playing, and for whatever reason, we'd just get mad at each other and argue over things that didn't make sense. We had begun to argue over things like accusing each other of having the other one's toy when we had the exact same toys, who grabbed a toy first, and just any little thing. And although I didn't like it, I thought that it was the correct way to handle things because it was always the way that Mom and Dad settled things. After they argued and yelled for a while, they would stomp off and go their separate ways and there was finally peace and quiet. So maybe if we argue long enough, then Twin will stomp off, and there would be peace.

Well, even if that was my plan, Mommy had a different one. Suddenly she would sometimes yell, "Y'all come here right now!" And I was scared instantly because that tone and type of call was never good. So we quickly obeyed, and the lashing began. "Y'all need to sit down somewhere and shut up." I was always told, "Stop standing there with that dumb grin on your face." And for the first time, she told Twin, "And you stop looking like a black butt just like your ugly black father."

Well, I didn't know whether to be offended or happy. Because my grin was just referred to as dumb, but to be told that you look like someone's black behind was just way too far. And the only thing that we could say to that was "yeeees" in unison and return to play.

What Mom had said had hurt us and we both cried that time. Why Mommy would call us those names was unknown to me, and I figured that I and Twin had better not argue anymore because there was no telling what she would call us next. Once we returned to our room, I told Twin, "I don't think that you look like a black butt," and she smiled in reply, and we wiped each other's faces and played some more, but without arguing. I felt a little closer to Twin after that moment, even if we were arguing just moments before. One thing about me and Twin was that we could argue heavily and play the next minute. It's just the way that it was. We didn't see ourselves as just sisters, but the bond was different because we were twins, and that meant that we were special because not everyone had a twin.

Although Mommy had grown angrier lately, whenever we got out of the apartment and went up on the hill, it lightened her mood. Although I despised that long walk, most of the time I wanted to take the walk at this point. Whatever it took to make

Mommy happy, I wanted it for her. We'd walk from Robinson Place to the hill, and then sometimes Mommy would leave us outside and be gone for a while and sometimes all day. And when she'd come back, her eyes would be different, and sometimes she would move slower. It was kind of scary, but at least she wasn't screaming and cussing and being mean to us. She was very calm, and the things that normally set her off just didn't seem to matter for a period of time.

Mom had this friend who seemed to make her happy sometimes. But he was a man, and he wasn't my daddy, so he already had two strikes against him. I didn't even know when and where he came from. Let's just call him Mr. B. Whenever Mr. B was around, he would take more of Mom's time and she wouldn't pay us any attention. He's one of the main people whom she would disappear for hours with.

I hated to see his face or even hear his name. At just the mention of his name, my face would bend up, as if I had just sucked on a mouthful of that disgusting candy called Lemonheads. He had never been mean to me or Twin, but the fact that he was taking up my mommy's time was enough for me to dislike him. Plus the very first time that I saw him I didn't understand why I got sick to my stomach. Before he ever said a word, I felt uneasy around him and didn't want any parts of him. And I didn't feel that way about any other male friend that Mommy had.

One sunny afternoon, Mom decided to take us on another walk. I didn't recall where it was, and as always, it was a long walk. So we ended up at Mr. B's apartment, and we were all sitting in Mr. B's bedroom. Twin and I were sitting on the floor at the end of the bed, watching something on TV. Mr. B began to tickle

Mom, or at least I assumed, because she kept rolling across the bed, giggling, "Stop...you' so crazy, and boy, stop playin'."

Well, I didn't think that it was so funny. I was hungry, and it was getting dark, and Mr. B didn't have a car, which meant we had to take the long, dark walk back home. So we sat there for hours, and Mom and Mr. B had left us in the bedroom and closed the bedroom door while they went into the living room. After we had complained and once we had run out of creative games to play, we drifted off to sleep on the floor. It was horribly uncomfortable, and there was no way that I or Twin would lay in some strange man's bed.

Once I woke up, Mommy said, "Come on, twins, lets go," and I looked at the red numbers on the alarm clock, and it was a little after two in the morning. I was simply horrified to walk out of this door, and as much as I didn't want to be at this man's apartment, I didn't want to walk home, either. And if Mr. B had any kind of conscience or concern, then he would've made a way for us to get home. But he didn't!

So we walked out into the night. It was a little chilly and extremely dark. There was one thing that I knew for sure, and that was that Twin was going to cry. And this time, I fully understood why. We were sleepy, and it was spooky and chilly outside. The sky was clear, and there was a bunch of stars in the sky. The air was crisp, and it smelled just like the city. I loved living in DC because it was always bustling and people were always in groups, hanging outside and just playing music and having fun. But there seemed to be an exception this particular night and in this particular neighborhood.

We continued to walk, and I kept hearing a rustling sound. I was a very observant child, and so I looked to the left, but the darkness made it impossible to see. Then I looked to my right and couldn't make anything out. I grabbed Twin's hand and squeezed tightly so that she would stop crying and feel safe, but I also did that to comfort myself.

All Mommy was saying was, "Y'all better hurry up before I leave y'all out here." That was just a mean thing to say, and I was sure that she didn't notice the look of horror that we had on our faces. Mommy never took note of our emotions. She never took the time to watch us and play with us or console us when we were frightened or unhappy. I thought that was a pretty mean thing to threaten us with.

I picked up the pace and dragged twin along. She looked at me when I looked back at her, and she smiled. Then both of us heard the rustling sound this time. We looked at each other, and our hands began to shake. This time when I looked to my left, there was a gentleman standing behind a bush next to a house. And as soon as I made eye contact with him, he put what appeared to be his finger to his lips and silently shushed me. I started to tell Mommy, but the funny thing was that when the stranger shushed me, he did it with something shiny and dark. I was unsure if it was his gloved hand, but the item was dark as he lifted it up but a quick glimmer of light from somewhere revealed a portion of it which made it appear to shine. Then as he moved forward from behind the bush, he tucked the black thing in the front of his pants and ran behind us, between two cars. I nearly urinated on myself, but we had to keep it moving.

When I looked to my right across the road, there was another strange man with what appeared to be a gun in his hand, staring across the street where the first dark stranger once stood. I could have screamed in horror, but I thought better of it and walked a little faster. I really didn't know what to do, and I just wanted to give up and flop to the ground, but I knew danger when I saw it, and danger was brewing right before our eyes. About five minutes later, there were about five or six gunshots, and I was so very relieved that we weren't as close as we were before. I wasn't any less afraid, and we moved like lightning once we heard the shots.

# *Life Lesson:*

Be sure to pay attention to how your children feel. Watch their movements, body language, and facial expressions because they may not be able to express how they feel about something. Spend time getting to know your children, and comfort them when they need you. Never threaten to leave or abandon your children. Whenever you threaten to abandon your children it causes them to fear and doesn't leave any room for them to grow and make mistakes. Every time that I made a mistake, I felt as if mom was going to leave us just like daddy did. Make your children feel safe when they are with you and allow them to make mistakes without punishment.

# BREAKFAST BEATING AND BULLYING

Once we arrived home safely and climbed into bed, I just couldn't sleep. Twin was fast asleep, and I lay there still shaking and horrified at the creepy, dark night that was outside of my window. I had never had a fear of the dark before, and I couldn't say that it was the dark that I was afraid of. Being caught in the middle of someone else's gunfight was not my idea of a happy time. Now it was my time to cry since there was no other time to do so.

I was in the third grade now, and school was getting tougher because home life was getting tougher. We had moved back in with Grandma for a reason unknown to me and Twin. Nevertheless, we were as happy as could be. We were with our grandma, and she always made everything better. I was having more trouble sleeping; therefore staying awake in school was challenging and was the result of my sleepless nights at home. Mommy was starting to disappear for quite a long time, just like Daddy. And even the kids at school were starting to talk about how they saw my mommy in different places, even though I wasn't seeing her.

Kids can be so cruel, and they were starting to tease me and Twin for everything. No matter how cute we looked going to school, certain kids talked about our clothes, and they just had to make our personal life known to everyone else. There was one girl in particular who never let me have any peace in my classroom. I had hair that was just below the halfway mark on my back; it was always done, and my clothes were always clean. True enough, I didn't have a wide variety of clothes, but they were always ironed and clean. My mom and grandma made sure that my long thick hair was beautifully laid down with the pressing comb and Blue Magic hair grease.

There was this one bully who made my already difficult life even more difficult. It wasn't that I was the least bit afraid of her. I was only in elementary school, and I was worn out. I was too tired to fight back, emotionally or physically. I was struggling to focus because I hadn't seen my mom in days, and I was worried and wondering if she was okay. I was kind of use to not seeing my daddy, but now Mommy was gone too. And when I lay in bed at night, I got physically sick with worry because I didn't know when and if they were coming back to get us. Daddy didn't live with us, so I was counting on Mommy to be there to make us feel safe and loved, and I was counting on her big time. I was becoming increasingly angry, and I couldn't specifically pinpoint just one thing. I was eight years of age and I already had puffy bags under my eyes.

One day in school, I was focusing on staying awake and completing a class work when the bully, let's call her T, stuck her foot out when I walked by her desk, and she whispered, "Your momma is a crackhead." I didn't know what *crack* was at that time, but the fact that she said anything about my mommy was enough for me. So as I walked back to my desk after sharpening my pencil, I quickly snatched everything that she had on her desk off and scattered it on the floor.

Of course, the teacher didn't hear her part of the disagreement, but she saw what I did and called me to the front of the class. I normally wasn't a mean child, and for some reason that I didn't really understand, I had become bitter, scared, and angry. I didn't care one bit about what I had just done. I went to the front of the class and took my consequence like a big girl and returned to my seat.

Now back when I was in elementary school, the teachers could spank the children that were in their care during the school day. And my teacher had four thick wooden rulers that were taped together with masking tape, and I received two whacks across my knuckles, and as I turned to T, I smiled and licked my tongue and took my rightful place in the classroom, at my desk. It was my very first punishment from a teacher since I had entered into elementary school. And it really hurt my virgin knuckles, but I wasn't going to let anyone see my pain.

So of course, later that night I cried as I lay in bed. I cried not only because my knuckles were still aching, but because my mommy wasn't there to hug me or put any ice on my hand. She wasn't there to ask how my day went and what struggles I had faced that day, and that was the hurtful part. At that point, I hadn't really eaten much in a couple of days. Not because we didn't have any food, because Grandma Rose and/or Nana made sure that we ate and were bathed and clothed daily, but I was so filled with grief and worry that I couldn't muster up any strength to even think about eating, although I was physically weak.

But I made it through another sleepless night, and when I had gotten out of bed to get dressed for school, Twin was already in the bathroom so I had to wait. Back in the day, we only had one bathroom, so waiting in line to use the bathroom was the only option. And peeing on yourself was definitely not an option. As we were getting dressed, Twin noticed that I was moving a little slower than usual. "You better hurry up so we won't be late."

I replied, a little more aggressively than I should have, "We live right across the street. We ain't never late so get outta my face."

When I saw the hurt on twin's face I quickly apologized, and as soon as I got the apology out of my mouth, we heard Mommy's voice. And we heard Grandma's too. "Liz, where have you been? Your kids have been worried sick about you and Kita won't even eat."

And it was shocking to hear Mommy's reply. "Then Kita must not be hungry." But the fact of the matter was that I was extremely hungry. Mom marched upstairs, and we both broke out in a short sprint so that we could hug her, but in midstride,

Mommy stopped us in our tracks and said, "Have y'all been eating breakfast and lunch at school?"

We replied in unison, "Yeeeees." I didn't know why we always dragged our words out as if we were singing.

"Then why are y'all so hungry?"

Twin said, "I'm not hungry, Mommy."

And I simply didn't answer because I didn't even know how to begin to make her understand that I was not hungry because there was a lack of food at school or at home, but simply because she'd been gone for days and I didn't know if she was coming back.

Whatever happened to her while she was gone, I wished that it would never happen again because she was pretty mad about something. She didn't even hug us, and she was yelling early in the morning because I was hungry. So she showed us out of the door and watched us until we crossed the street to walk to the school. And we immediately went to the cafeteria to eat, just as we did every morning that we had school. Mom was angry and a little smelly, so I was hoping that she was going to calm down and take a shower. I wondered if she had taken a bath while she was away because I had never smelled her like she was at that time.

Now that Mommy was back, I felt a lot better, and I was finally able to eat something. We had just placed our backpacks on the bench and were heading to the line to be served when all of a sudden Mommy came into the cafeteria with the infamous white whooping belt in her hand. Whenever any of the children came over to Grandma's house and they needed to be disciplined, there was a white belt that we were all too familiar with. The belt was thick, and it started out as a white belt but had peeled, and the buckle had been broken off. But it was very obvious that just because the belt wasn't in its original state, it was still good enough to be used. There were times where we hid that thing, and Grandma would somehow find it every time. But there was one time that we hid it behind the radiator and hoped that it wouldn't catch fire.

When Mommy walked into the cafeteria, I saw her, and she looked furious. And how she was able to find us among a group of one hundred students, I still can't figure out to this day. Nevertheless, she headed straight for us as we walked out into the aisle to go to the entrance of the serving line. Again, she didn't greet us with a hello, a hug, or any other show of affection, and she walked straight up to us and yelled, "Why haven't y'all been eating breakfast?"

And we were too embarrassed and afraid to answer immediately so we did what twins did quite often; we turned and looked at each other and sang in unison, "We haaaaave been eating breakfast."

But that wasn't good enough because she whooped us right in the cafeteria in front of all of our friends and classmates. And I still don't understand why you would ask a child a question when you know that no matter their response, you're going to whoop them anyway. I couldn't concentrate the rest of the day. I was extremely embarrassed and hurt that Mommy didn't even listen to us and she whooped us for no reason. And from that day on, that's all that the other kids needed to see in order to pick on us even more. They were already following us home after school, calling our mom a crackhead, pulling our hair, and now they'd already started to laugh at us because we got whooped in school. This was so far the most humiliating day of my young life.

And when the school day was over, I was so relieved because there was no one else to pick on me. It would be just me and my twin, and we could live together in peace and harmony. Although we argued sometimes, we never called each other negative names and we never talked bad about each other. I wanted to scream and cry and just shrink away from everything, but Twin was being teased too, and someone had to protect her.

Twin and I met up at the side of the school so that we could walk across the street together, and of course, the usual bully, T, was right behind us. But this time, she had some additional people to add to the torment. They followed behind us and yelled, "Black ugly twins, black ugly twins, y'all stupid, and y'all momma on drugs. And y'all ain't got no daddy." As much as I wanted to turn around and throw a glass bottle and split somebody's head to the white meat, I didn't because it wouldn't make anything better. I grabbed Twin's hand, and we held each other's hands real tight until we disappeared into the house in hopes of drowning out the entire day.

When we got home and saw that Mommy was there it made the day a lot better, although she was the cause of our anguish. I threw my backpack down and sighed heavily, sat down at the table, and wept. Normally, I'd spend time at night when I couldn't sleep and would just weep silently. But that particular day was just unbearable, and I felt like I couldn't take it any longer. I was tired of the teasing and the kids walking pass my desk and pulling my hair and embarrassing me in front of everyone.

Mom came walking down the stairs and cheerfully said, "Hey, twins, y'all got any homework?" And when she saw me crying, she said, "I don't know what you're still crying for. I bet you'll eat from now on."

## *Life Lesson:*

Bullying is not right and should not be tolerated. Bullies become bullies because they are unhappy with themselves and aim to cause the next person to hurt, just as they are hurting. Bullying is a *cowardly* act! A bully is defined as a blustering, quarrelsome, overbearing person who habitually badgers and intimidates smaller or weaker people (Dictionary.com). Bullying can be physically hitting someone and verbally or emotionally tormenting someone by teasing them, calling them names, throwing things at them, and even following them home.

Parents should talk to their children daily and ask them how their day went, and they will surely tell you. Spend time talking and listening to your children and learning them. This will enable the parent to recognize different problems, and it is the parent's responsibility to provide the protection and help that the child needs. Children know exactly what's wrong, and they don't always know how to articulate what they are feeling. So creating a safe and positive environment for children to express themselves is very important. Ask questions and allow the child to answer them without getting angry or punishing them. If they are being bullied, get them some help and report bullies to their schools or the police.

# MISSING PERSON

I didn't know what to make of life at that point. Now I was so consumed with the question, "Is everybody's life this way?" After that last fiasco in the cafeteria, I just wanted everyone to forget about it so that I could get back to a somewhat normal life, if there was such a thing. I think you call it wishful thinking. For example, one day I was sitting in class and was trying to do my work when the bully walked by and yanked my long ponytail really hard. And she was so sneaky that the teacher never saw her do anything. I slammed my pencil down and quickly got up out of my seat as she was walking back to her seat and shoved her as hard as I possibly could. I got back to my seat faster than lightning, and the teacher thought that she had tripped.

This girl got on my nerves so bad, and she never gave me a break. She followed me home every single day, and I was rapidly growing weary of her and her efforts to make my life miserable. And now that she was constantly bothering me, there were more kids following her unhealthy pattern. There was one boy in particular, named J, who began to talk about the way that me and my twin looked. J and another boy had begun to call me and Twin rude and negative names, and they would say that we looked like monkeys, and they helped other kids notice that twin and I weren't very rich either. They talked about our clothes and how we wore the same outfits over and over again. Although it was the truth, our clothes were always clean and ironed. But it still hurt to see other kids all pointing and laughing.

Not all kids were mean and hurtful, and we had some really true and loyal friends that were never mean and nasty and didn't tease us because of the life that we were forced to live. One of my closest friends that truly had a major impact on my life was a girl named Tamara. She was the nicest person, and she was always there to say "Kita, it's okay. They are so stupid." She was a great listener and was always willing to play with me on the playground, and she never switched on me. She was one of the girls who gave me hope that not everyone in the world was mean and rude. And to this very day, I think of her often and have spoken blessings over her life. I pray that God will bless her and her family abundantly.

I loved to go to school, and learning was super fun. I wanted to do anything to get out of the house and take my mind off of my mom and dad being gone. I didn't like playing with dolls, but I loved to play basketball, listen to music, and play musical instruments, and participating in track and field. Books were my favorite thing in the whole world. I loved to read because I could get away from reality for a while, and I loved to learn new words and play word games. I read all types of books and was easily entertained with them. Between my twin and my books, I was never bored.

I can vividly remember one day when we had arrived home from school, which was right across the street, and Grandma was on the phone. Normally, we weren't allowed to just stand around in grown-folks business. Not even while they were having a phone conversation. It was our duty as children to stay in a child's place. And that included speaking when we were spoken to, obeying quickly when we were told to do something, not back-talking, stomping off, or slamming anything that we didn't pay for. All of these rules made childhood seem so hard, but now I know that it was for our own good.

I heard Grandma say, "I'd like to report a missing person." And that immediately got my attention, or as my grandma would put it, my antenna went straight up. And the weird thing about it was that Twin heard it too, but it didn't seem to intrigue her one bit.

I never understood how we were conceived together, shared the placenta together, were birthed and raised together yet have two totally different ways of dealing with things. My mind analyzed everything. I thought long and hard about everything, and I noticed people's facial expressions and was very observant of the things going on around me. And Twin seemed to be just the opposite. She cried for what she said was no apparent reason, and she didn't pay attention to detail. She acted as if nothing affected her and if she remembered none of the negative events that took place in our lives.

So I brushed off the comment that I had heard and continued to prepare to do homework. But I couldn't seem to focus until my mind processed Grandma's missing-person statement. This is my brain's process: as soon as I heard the statement, I silently asked, *Why would Grandma report someone missing whom she doesn't know? Why would she care to report some random person missing? Furthermore, who was it that was missing?* I do know that Grandma Rose was faithful in watching her daytime soap operas and the news, and I was pretty much the same way. It was a way that I could sit up under my grandma and just chill out. We didn't have much conversation going on during this time because in between her nodding and denying that she was ever asleep and her commenting on how foolish the world was and her infatuation with Victor Newman, we were just enjoying the sound of the television. I do know that when I did watch the news and see that a person was missing, in most cases, some sort of abduction took place.

And then I thought silently again and continually wondered who would snatch up a grown person. And then the light bulb came on! I put two and two together and thought that Mommy had been gone for more than four days, and I concluded that she had to have been talking about Mommy. And I narrowed this down because Mommy hadn't been seen for close to a week and Grandma had been fussing more than usual about Mom being missing. There were times where she would disappear for two days or so, but never seven days. And that's when my little world came crashing down. Sorrow overtook me, and all I could do was worry and cry. I didn't sleep for two more days.

I laid tossing and turning all night long, even though I had to go to school. To confirm my suspicions, I confronted Grandma and asked her straight up, "Is my mommy missing?" And Grandma, like any other loving grandma, heard the concern in my voice and saw the weariness on my face and sadly replied, "She'll be back soon."

I didn't think that Twin knew what was going on, so I thought it would only be fair if I helped her to understand before she overheard it from Grandma or maybe even saw it on the news. And of course, it rocked her world more than it did mine. But I had my time to sob and try to begin to hope and heal, and now I had to make sure that Twin was protected because there was no one else to do it when Grandma wasn't around. I am unsure as to what happened with the missing person report because I didn't understand if a report had been filed or if Grandma was talking to a relative on the phone. I just knew that I wanted everything and everybody to be alright.

# *Life Lesson:*

People are wired differently, and at a young age, I knew that I was very observant, and I thought over every situation long and hard. My deep thoughts kept me awake at night, and very little was done to calm my fears and thoughts. Parents are responsible for creating a place of refuge for their children. A place of refuge emotionally and physically is a major part of developing a child. Especially in a child's early years, parents need to be present to assist in their child's development.

Parents should be present to instill values in their children and to assist them in figuring out what their gifts are and to set goals. Then they should be present to help them to accomplish their goals and to become confident in who they are. And it is important to remember that this positive growth and development takes more than just "being there," but in being effective. Speak good things to your children and be positive. Create a well-balanced life where correction and love are both a consistent part of life.

# THE STRANGER
# WHO KNEW ME

By this time, Mommy still hadn't been seen, at least by us, in nine days. And when I went to school one bright Monday morning, the bully, T, made it her personal business to wait until recess when there were at least ten other students around when she said, "Guess what?"

I didn't care to speak to her, let alone play some stupid guessing game with her. So I said, "Get outta my face, I don't wanna play no guessing game with you." One thing that I was never good at was pretending or faking. No one ever had to guess how I felt about something. I didn't know what name to give it when I was younger, but now I can say that I am and have always been totally transparent. I wanted the bully to know exactly how I felt about her. She tortured me every day that she could, about anything that she could think of and I was almost fed up with her. She was definitely the ring leader of the teasing and heartache that I experienced. And my reply only made her mad, and so of course, there was more to come.

"Well, I don't care, and I ain't goin' nowhere" was her reply.

At this point, I normally just walked away and let her look stupid as she stood in place and argued alone. But that day and moment was not the day that I was going to take her mess! I walked closer to her and dared her to say another word or I would swell her lips up. I was not a violent child who liked to start trouble, and she had no idea that my god brothers taught me to fight and that I wasn't afraid of her; I was just too weary to battle with her.

For a split second, her eyes grew wider than her head, and because there was now a crowd, she had to quickly recover. "Dats why I saw your crackhead momma yesterday, and she was all funky and lookin' all nasty."

I felt like I wanted to shrink away and disappear right then. Besides the cafeteria beating, I had never felt more embarrassed in my life. And I knew that there was a possibility that it was true because I hadn't seen Mommy. But at least she wasn't actually missing. There was no way that I could defend myself against that, and I felt the hurt all on my face. And for a brief moment the bully, T, saw it too because her face quickly had a moment of sorrow and regret on it. But it didn't last nearly as long as I would've wanted. Since there was a crowd around laughing hysterically and saying, "Oooh, oooooh," she had to finish it out with, "And y'all probably don't have no father either."

All I could say was, "Everybody has a father, stupid." I walked off with my head held high and I went into the girl's bathroom, and I cried until I didn't think that I had any more tears. Once I got myself together, I went back to class and tried to stay awake, and I watched the clock diligently with hopes that it would somehow move to three o'clock right at that moment. And just as I thought, T and her new recruits followed behind me and Twin on the way home with a new song. They danced across the street behind us and sang in unison, "Y'all ain't got no daddy, and your momma is a crackhead, and y'all are so ugly and stupid."

When we got home, it was such a relief for me and Twin to just kick back and play with our toys and enjoy some peace. Mommy showed up a couple of hours after we got home, and this time she plopped down on the couch, and we were glued to her side. It looked like she had two brown long sleeves on because we wrapped our arms around hers and just enjoyed her presence.

I finally said, "Mommy, all the kids at school are calling you a crackhead and calling us ugly and stupid and black. What is a crackhead?"

And she coldly replied "Girl, those doggon' kids don't know what they are talking about. Tell them to kiss your black you know what the next time they have somethin' to say."

And I was elated because normally we were taught not to say those kinds of words. My mom's language was explicit. She taught us not to say the same words, and other times, she encouraged us to say them. It was so confusing, being a child. And I suddenly remembered that Twin cussed when we were a little younger, and she didn't get a beating or punished for it. So I experienced my very first aha moment. Finally, I fell fast asleep since I saw Mommy and I knew that she was safe.

But my sleep didn't last very long. I woke up nearly two hours later because I could've sworn that the bully and the others were standing over my bed and pointing, laughing, and singing, "Y'all ain't got no daddy, and your momma is a crackhead , and y'all are so ugly and stupid." I jumped up out of my sleep with tears in my eyes and my fists balled tightly, but it was pitch black, and there was no one standing over me. I looked across the small room and saw Twin lying fast asleep in her bed.

I couldn't really sleep after that, so I tossed and turned constantly until the alarm went off. Although my slim little body was weary, I went to school with a new attitude. I wasn't gonna let anyone tell me anything negative today because Mommy said, "Tell them to kiss your behind." So I was excited because I had something to fight back with.

The ring leader bully didn't come to school that day, so I didn't have to use what Mommy said. The rest of the week passed by, and I didn't have to curse anybody out. It always amazed me how some people didn't do negative things as long as the ring leader didn't do it. It had been one of the most peaceful weeks at school so far.

Bright and early on Saturday, Grandma woke us up and we brushed our teeth, got dressed and ate our famous bowl of oatmeal with raisins and toast. Then it was off for a day with Grandma in the blue Thunderbird.

We loved our trips with Grandma. It didn't matter where we were going, we just wanted to go. We knew that we would look cute, no one would be teasing us, and we were going to eat and have fun. We especially loved our trips with Grandma to the grocery store because she always went into the Safeway or Giant to get a pack of hotdogs. But we came out with way more than she went in for and that always benefited us.

We sat in the backseat with our deck of cards and a coloring book with crayons as we headed to some unknown destination. It started to pour down raining, and I thought that I would have a little fun with Twin. For a while, we played the buggy game, and that was whenever you saw a Volkswagen beetle you'd have to be the first to yell "Punch buggy, no punch back" in order to get the point. Well, after a while, that got boring, so we began to get restless, and I blew my breath on the window to fog it up and thought that it was a good idea to write the word *help* where I had fogged the window up. And I was so brilliant that I wrote it backward so that the people passing by could read it. I was always so amazed at my talents and was so proud of these crafty things that no one else seemed to think of.

We sat in the back, and I snickered and snickered until a state trooper turned his pretty lights on and summoned Grandma to the side of Interstate 95. Well, I still thought that it was rather funny until the trooper walked Grandma around to the right rear passenger window where he pointed to the window and she saw the world *help* written there. And what was even more shocking to me was that Grandma snatched me out of that car. I finally knew what whiplash was. She whooped me until my butt cheeks burned, and I think they may have swelled to a different size.

There was also such a thing as child abuse, and I was wondering when the nice officer was going to make Grandma aware of that. It didn't occur to me right away that he had pulled Grandma over because he thought that we were possibly being abducted, like we thought that Mommy had been. I thought that he had stopped us because he thought that it was funny and that I was a clever little kid. It seemed like she had beat me for an hour. And trust me, the pain wasn't worth it!

After that incident, we rode down to Eastover to the post office where, back in the day, people actually frequented the post office because there was no paying your bills online. Grandma parked the car and helped us out of the car, and as we walked to the front of the post-office entrance, there was a dirty, homeless man sitting on the sidewalk and leaning against the blue mailbox that was out front. And as we walked by, I inhaled and almost threw up. This man smelled so bad and Twin looked at me and made the stinky face. (The stinky face was the one where all of your facial features come together in the middle of your face and you scrunch your face up).

I felt deeply sad for the man. His eyes were half-closed, and he kept scratching his neck and chest. His eyes were sad like mine, and his lips were all white and cracked. He was definitely a pitiful site to behold. We continued into the post office, and Grandma finished her business, and as we headed back out and passed by the man, I looked into his eyes, and immediately my heart sank. There was something so familiar about this man, and the more that I stared, the more Grandma summoned me to keep up. I said okay to grandma and looked at the man one last time.

Because I had been such an observant child, I never forgot a face. And although I didn't immediately recognize this man, there was something that was way too familiar about him. It was then that I realized not only did I feel sorry for this man because he didn't have a home, food, clothes and soap and water, but more sad at the fact that I realized that he was my daddy. And that wasn't even the saddest part, but when I let go of Grandma's hand and ran back to hug him, he didn't even know who I was. It had been at least two or three months since we had seen him, and he looked nothing like he did the last time. I ran up to him and grabbed his neck, despite his look and the rank odor that came from him.

Grandma yelled after me and walked quickly over to me and Daddy and pried me from around his neck. I had never ever seen Grandma this upset with me, but it was my daddy. She yelled, "Girl, you know better than to run off and run to a stranger."

And I assumed that she didn't hear me the first time that I said it, so I repeated, "Grandma, it's my daddy."

Grandma was in utter shock, and Daddy looked up at me and mumbled some incoherent statement at me and that hurt. He shoved me away from him and continued to mumble something that I didn't understand. Whatever it was that he was trying to convey to me was not understood by me, nor was it well received. I can remember being short of breath and just standing there crying because he really didn't know who we were. I grabbed Twin and told her to say something to him, especially since Mommy says that Twin looked exactly like her "black ugly father." Twin couldn't believe her eyes either, and she couldn't muster up the strength to say anything.

Grandma couldn't say much, and she quickly grabbed us by the hand, and we left Daddy sitting there against the mailbox looking helpless and smelling horrible. Although Grandma was mad at me, and I never told her how I felt, I'm sure that she saw the look of horror and overwhelming sadness that we had on our little faces. I couldn't stop crying and feeling hopeless, and that was because I couldn't help Daddy. I didn't think that anybody could've helped him.

She took us home and tried to lighten the mood by picking up our cousin Lil B, and she took us to Hains Point at East Potomac Park. Being with our big cousin Lil B was always a great time because we were carefree and always laughing about something.

She took us to this park quite often because she knew that it was our favorite place to go and she always allowed us to just run wild and have a good time. We really enjoyed climbing up on this huge metal hand that came out of the ground. Grandma was faithful in making our favorite bologna-and-cheese sandwiches with mayo and black pepper, and she cut them diagonally just like we liked them, and we had a sandwich bag of ranch corn chips with a couple of little Hugs juices.

It didn't erase the images in my mind of my daddy resting on a sidewalk strung out, but Grandma really made me feel a lot better. It took my mind off of the catastrophe for a while. Up until that point in my life, I had experienced more sadness and heartache than I did happy times. The older I got, the more difficult it became to manage this sadness. I didn't how to control it, but I became angrier because of the life that I was forced to live, and it didn't seem like anyone other than Grandma cared to make it better.

# *Life Lesson:*

Create happy moments and experiences so that your children will have something to remember. With life comes challenges and sometimes those challenges cause unhappy experiences, and it is important to let the good times outweigh the bad. As a parent, you definitely have control over what your children experience. Although it takes a village to raise a child, and you may have a great support system, it is the parents' ultimate responsibility to raise their children and allow the rest of the village to do what they are intended to do, which is assist.

A child should not have to fight an adult's battle and make excuses for why they are present and why they allow an addiction to take control of their lives and dictate what they can or can't do. Addiction not only affects the person who is addicted, but anyone who cares about and loves them.

# UNSAFE, YET SECURE

I was about nine years old now when we had moved out of Grandma's house and moved across the street on the same side of the street as our school into a building called the high rise. Our elementary school was at the top of the hill, and the high rise was just midway down the hill. We lived on the ninth floor, and to us, that was pretty high up. It was a nice apartment because it was ours—well, it was really Mommy's.

I must admit that the building itself was spooky. The halls were always dimly lit, and the stairwells were lonely, cold and creepy. It always crept us out to get on the elevator whenever it worked or to walk up the stairs to get to our apartment. I often overheard the adults telling stories of who was robbed in the hallways or elevators and who was found on the bottom floor dead. And quite frankly it was spooky, even in broad daylight. There were no windows in the building, except the ones in the individual apartments.

It was one sunny, beautiful day when we arrived at our apartment and Twin and I were sitting on the balcony just looking at the big field across the street, because our balcony was in the back of the building. We looked right out at the back of Hart Junior High School, and we couldn't wait until we were old enough to go there. I had always hoped that when we did go to Hart, things would be better than they were at Draper. I'd hoped that the kids were less cruel and more mindful of other people's feelings. Mommy said that she would be right back and that she was going up the hill to Grandma's house to pick up something. And when she had returned, we wondered why she was knocking on the door when it was her apartment and she had a key. She taught us not to answer the door for anyone, so whoever it was would have to just knock until their knuckles bled.

We heard Lil B yelling through the door, "Twins, open the door."

Being my playful self, I went to the door and looked out of the peephole and yelled back, "No, we can't answer the door for nobody."

That followed with some snickering from me and Twin as we slumped over and covered our mouths to prevent him from hearing us laugh. And this time, he didn't answer back. I knew that this was not normal because I, twin, and Lil B always played and joked around, and he didn't sound too happy. So I planned to suffer the consequences later, and I opened the door. He was completely out of breath, but he managed to get out, "Something is wrong with Grandma."

So we locked the door and ran like lightning up the hill and across the street where the ambulance was pulling away, and all that I could see was my grandma being loaded into the ambulance and them whisking her away. I was horrified beyond belief, and so I began to cry, yell, and jog after the ambulance and saying, "Please stop...please, Grandma, please come back." But they ignored me and drove away with my grandma.

I fell to my knees in the grass and couldn't understand nor believe what had just happened. Once I realized that I was on my knees, with Lil B and Twin repeating "Get up Kita. Get up," I got up and ran as fast I could into the house to see what in the world was going on. I heard Mommy on the phone telling someone that Grandma had a stroke, and I had no earthly idea what that was. And the thought that I may not see her again was unfathomable.

Although previously I felt as if my world had crumbled, now my foundation had been rocked. Beside my biological grandma (Rose) and my second grandma, or as I like to call her, Nana, I didn't feel like I had anyone else to protect me.

Grandma was in the hospital for a couple of days, and we did get the chance to go and see her. And since Mommy had to be home with us now, it was a very interesting couple of days. Mommy walked us everywhere she went. We'd wake up early and be out of the house sometimes at nine o'clock in the morning, and we'd be on the hill playing and wouldn't see her until later that night.

One day in particular was especially scary for both me and twin. We were outside playing with our god brother, and we were kneeling down at the corner right across the street from the front entrance of our school trying to decide who would be the person who was considered to be it in our game of tag. And what I personally thought was the coolest thing happened. Three or four police vans, or what we commonly referred to in the hood as jumpouts, came cruising around the corner.

At first they drove pass us slowly, and I thought nothing more of it and finally assumed that they were gone. About two minutes later, policemen were coming from everywhere with huge rifles drawn. There were so many officers that it was truly fascinating until I realized that whenever police were around that it wasn't a good thing. They looked like they were on the SWAT team, with their helmets and vests.

Two of the officers led the pack and ran swiftly past us, and one of them trampled right over me. I was officially horrified and didn't know where to go from there. Our god brother and Twin were frozen stiff and looked at me with sheer horror on their faces. I was temporarily discombobulated and was trying to get up and shake myself off. I don't know how I stepped in his way, but he obviously didn't see me because he knocked me over and stepped right on me. But then another officer came by and scooped me up off of the ground and pointed to a place where the three of us could go and hide. So we did as we were instructed to do. But what was weird was that the nice officer took his time to make sure that we were okay. It had been my first time having such a close encounter with real policeman, and from that moment on, I have had a deep love for policemen and women.

Anyway, we went to our hiding spot and watched as they kicked a couple of people's doors in and entered their homes with their guns drawn. It was horrifying because I didn't know where to run or what to do because Mommy was gone and I didn't know if she was in one of those houses or if they were looking for her because she was a missing person. I wondered if this was what happened when people were reported missing around the world. Would there be some Special Forces team that would come in and kick down doors until they located the missing person? And once the policemen left, who would be there to protect us and tell us that everything is going to be okay?

I didn't feel secure when I had been run over, but for some odd reason I was always looking for security in my life. By the time I was 9 years of age, I thought that I had experienced enough scary situations and trauma that would last a life time. I was growing increasingly scared and I wanted my mommy or daddy to come home and pick me up and hug me just like that police officer did. And being carried off to safety was something that I longed for.

## *Life Lesson:*

Provide some stability for your children. It is vital that both parents be a consistently present part of their children's lives. Parents should be present and available to calm their children's fears. Parents should be present to be able to talk to their children and see what their fears are and help them to overcome them. When children are around their family and their parents, they should be provided with maximum safety and security. Children should feel like their parents will do any and everything to make them feel secure with themselves and their surroundings.

# NO FEAR AT GUNPOINT

We wandered the neighborhood for hours, and we had a habit of running in and out of Nana's house while Mommy was away. Her disappearances were unfortunately so normal now that I was getting the hang of being on my own. It was the fact that although any adult in the neighborhood could whoop us, I was more afraid of my mom whoopin' us. The other adults whoopins just didn't feel the same. I can say that now that I'm grown!

One thing that was never up for negotiation was the fact that when the streetlights came on, we were supposed to be at somebody's front door or a serious whoopin' was in our immediate future. So we did make sure that we were in front of Nana's house, even if mommy wasn't there.

One day, Mommy didn't show up when the streetlights came on, and everyone was starting to go inside, but we didn't have anywhere to go. Nana told us to come on inside and eat, but I just couldn't muster up the appetite because I was so nervous and scared of what could be happening to my parents. I never saw Daddy, and whenever Mommy was around, she was moving and talking slow or she was very mean. Her eyes were always red, and she looked like she wanted to go to sleep all of the time. Her words were slurred, and she acted like she didn't care about anything.

After I had done all of the crying that I could do that night, Nana told us to get in the chair. Now to some, that may mean nothing. But the blue chair was a total nightmare. Whenever we would cry because Mommy was leaving, Nana would make the both of us sit in that chair together until she said that it was time to move. And she made *the best* spaghetti in the whole wide world. But even though she had made a big pot this particular night, I still couldn't eat because I was sad that Mommy was gone. All I could think about was Mommy sitting in someone's house and the police kicking the door down with their big guns in their hands.

I watched the clock and begged Nana to let us sit on the bench in front of the house to wait for Mommy. I hated the fact that she was so weary from us crying, but I didn't know what else to do. I never meant to get on Nana's nerves, and I was even more upset that Mommy would constantly leave Nana to look after us, knowing that we would cry and make Nana tired of us too. We didn't want her to get mad at us and stop loving or looking after us. She finally let us sit outside on the bench because other people from the neighborhood were out there. And before we knew it, it was just after two o'clock in the morning.

Throughout the day, people had stopped by Grandma's house to see if she was home so that Twin and I could go home, but to no avail. Finally, someone got in touch with my grandmother, and she said that she wasn't getting out of bed to come and get us. And I knew at times that Grandma was tired of us, but I didn't know that she was really, really tired of us. So we had to walk from Nana's house around the corner to Grandma's house. It was pitch black and even the street lights weren't enough to illuminate the neighborhood to the point where we would feel safe enough to walk home without being horrified. And this time, Mommy wasn't with us. I never knew how dark it actually was because we were always in the house at this time of the night.

Once we got past the school, it was eerily dark. And we held each other tight and shook the entire way there. I couldn't see my hand in front of my face, so we walked slowly. There was no telling who was lurking behind a bush or at one of the end housing units. Our duplexes were attached, so I knew that there wasn't anyone in between them. But we did have to walk near the alley behind our house, and there was a dark field back there also. I was afraid to talk because if someone was hiding behind a house or bush like before, then I surely thought that they would come out to get us or maybe shoot us. We were scared to walk, talk, and even breathe. But we had to make it around the corner.

By the time we made it to the door, we had to stand there shaking and knocking on the door and waiting for Grandma to come and open the door. We were deathly afraid, and when Grandma did finally come and open the door, I was so horrified that I had urinated in my pants and couldn't sleep for two days after that. I lay in bed for hours just trembling and worrying, and when the sun rose and Grandma had fixed us some breakfast, I couldn't even eat. I felt weak and feeble again, and I was literally worried sick. I had wondered what Daddy was doing too. The question that bothered me the most was, "Why doesn't Mommy or Daddy want us?"

After a couple of days had passed, Mommy came back home, and just like last time, she was really stinky and her hair wasn't done, and although I was young, I knew that she looked a mess and that this was not normal. She picked us up from Grandma's house, and we walked back across the street to the high rise. I was so very happy to see Mommy, but she didn't seem all that happy to see us. Although it didn't feel like Mommy loved us, we still loved her and desired to be around her.

After a couple of days had gone by, Mommy had just gotten off of work, and she went to cash her check. She was gone so much that I didn't see how she even had or kept a job. I know that she and Grandma worked at Howard University in the registration office, and that was a seasonal job. We got to the front door of the high rise and entered into the dimly lit lobby and waited for the creepy elevator. We stepped in, and Mommy pushed the button to our floor. It stopped two floors away from ours, and a strange hooded man got on with us. We scooted a little closer to Mommy, and she put an arm around us. When we heard the *ding*, I was so happy because we could leave this stranger behind. He didn't say anything, and he didn't even look our way.

By the time we went to step off of the elevator, the hooded stranger had placed a small shiny black handgun to my mommy's head and calmly said, "Give me your money."

Twin immediately started to cry, and I held her close to me, hoping that she would quiet down and not cause this man to get upset and shoot Mommy.

He kept the gun pressed on the side of mommy's head and looked at twin and said, "Twin, shut your little butt up." He turned his face back to Mommy and said, "Liz, gimme da money."

And at that moment, any trace of fear vanished from Mommy's face and anger took over. She raised her hand and pushed the gun away from her head and looked the stranger straight in the eyes and said, "Lee, you betta get this gun outta my face and get outta here."

I thought at that point that Mommy was what the old folks use to call plum crazy. I had never seen anyone push a gun away from their head and tell the man in control of the gun that they weren't going to do anything. Even on TV, I hadn't witnessed such bravery. And though I thought that it was a brave move, I thought that it was a foolish one also. I didn't know much, but I knew that it wasn't a wise move to disobey the man with the gun, especially when you're on the barrel end. I was even more frightened because Mommy knew the robber. I wondered if this is the guy who caused her to be a missing person or if she had done something personally to him to make him want to take her money or shoot her and us. If so, I didn't like him very much.

And then my light bulb came on. I knew exactly who this Lee was, and he quickly confirmed my suspicions by removing his hood and bandana from his face. I had never even seen him put the bandana on his face. From the time that he stepped onto the elevator, I was looking his way, but I guess that I just didn't notice that he had a bandana on.

He looked directly at me and twin, and a brief moment of sorrow crossed his face, and once he recovered from that, he put the gun back up to Mommy's head and said, "I ain't playin' with you. Give me your money. I know you just got paid today."

Mommy replied, "Like I said before, you betta get that gun out of my face and go ahead, Lee."

I and twin were horrified at what could happen at any moment. We didn't know if the gun had bullets in it or not, but Mommy didn't seem afraid at all. Mommy grabbed our hands, and we walked right out of the elevator as Lee called behind us. I was so worried that he would shoot us in the back or in the back of the head as we walked away.

I had so many mixed feelings, and I didn't know if I should've been proud of Mommy for protecting us or mad at her for the fact that he could've shot any one of us at any time. At my age, I had learned very quickly to count my blessings and enjoy any and every good moment that I experienced, instead of worrying about what could've happened.

We were probably nine years of age at the time of this incident, and I didn't know how to handle life. There were so many things going on, and I had a lot of questions about life that weren't answered, questions involving my body development, school, how to deal with bullies, and the list went on and on. I had started to have these feelings in my body and an interest in boys, and there was no one to answer the questions that I had. Grandma and Nana were around, and my godmothers (Nana's daughter's) were also a wonderful part of my life. I don't know why, but I was embarrassed to ask anyone else.

I overheard a lot of the other girls at school talking about how they sat down with their moms and sometimes both of their parents, for those who were fortunate enough to have both of their parents living in the home, and they talked about sex, lying, drugs, what to do in life and what not to do. I became increasingly angry because I didn't have the same thing. I wasn't mad at any one particular thing or one particular person. I just know that

I was jealous, and that was causing me to become angrier. I and twin were the same age, so of course, we probably had the same questions.

My mom's disappearances and long breaks were growing more frequent, and at the age of nine, we were in desperate need of some guidance. I was hurting inside, and I didn't know what to do to release all of these feelings. But the only thing that I did and could do was hold it all inside and hope that one day there would be some help from Mommy or Daddy or from someone who was willing to just listen to me. I had experienced a lot, and I just wanted to talk and for someone to just listen.

There had been times in the past where I had been happy every once in a while, but I had gotten to the point where I was angry or extremely sad all the time. I couldn't stop thinking about all of the things that I didn't have and all of the things that I wanted. Those things were love, attention, safety, and my fears to go away, appreciation, peace, boundaries, and happiness. I wanted to feel like I was worth something and that I was needed and wanted. I had become so uninterested with life, and when I had gotten older, I figured that I was in a state of depression.

I attended the entire fifth and sixth grade school years without smiling. I had sunken so low and didn't even see the point in smiling or faking like I was happy. And to prevent from faking, I just didn't smile. I didn't find anything funny and there was absolutely nothing to smile about.

My fifth grade teacher Ms. Haynes was a great influence in my life. She was always so straightforward and soft-spoken, and she did her best to counsel me and try to bring some sort of guidance to my life, but to no avail. I sank deeper into a sad state and felt like I was unwanted, not good enough and not loved. I felt like no one but Twin wanted me around, and she felt the same, which is why we were so close growing up. We couldn't help each other because we had the same questions and concerns, and neither of us understood life enough to know what to do. And to this day, we are extremely close.

Ms. Haynes threatened me daily that if I didn't at least fake a smile, I couldn't go outside for recess. And for the entire fifth grade, I didn't have a recess. I had never been good at faking any thing. If something wasn't funny, then I didn't laugh; if something made me afraid, then I would show that I was afraid, etc.

I didn't know how to pull myself out of this sad and lonely state. I just knew that I wanted my mommy and daddy to come back around so that I could apologize for whatever it was that I and twin did to cause them to argue all the time and then slowly just fade from our lives. And because of the absence of my parents, there was a void that no one else could fill.

I am so very grateful that my grandma and Nana were there, and I would never decrease what they have done for us and what they sacrificed for us. For all of the times they spent dressing us, bathing and feeding us, making sure that we had food and snacks, and making sure that we had a roof over our heads, I am forever grateful! I have a special love and place for them in my heart and life.

During the summer after fifth grade, I still hadn't found the joy or happiness that I longed for, and I went into sixth grade without finding it. So the bullying somehow found its way back to us, and the same ring leader wanted us to be sure that we knew that she was the ring leader. She continued to follow us home, and this was about the fourth school year that this went on. All I knew was anger, and I missed out on another school year of recess because of my lack of joy and inability to fake it. This time, it was my sixth-grade teacher Mrs. Barino whom I simply adored just as much as Ms. Haynes. Both teachers knew my mommy very well because they had taught most of my family members when they were in school.

## *Life Lesson:*

Oftentimes, an addict has a support system, which consists of family members, friends, and other people who love them and care about their well-being. And oftentimes these villages of supporters take on the responsibility that the addict left behind. Addicts don't intentionally neglect their children and other duties, but being addicted to drugs, alcohol, sex, or any other thing can cause the addict to simply lose focus of all of their other responsibilities. In turn, this forces the addict's family and friends to pick up the pieces and attempt to create a life of normalcy for their children.

There is no comfort, support, refuge, peace, and love like that of a parent, and each parent contributes differently to their children. Parents should never think of just themselves. The moment that their child is conceived and they are made aware that the mother is pregnant, proper preparations should be made then. Parents should discuss how they plan to provide for the child and meet the child's physical and emotional needs.

It is a difficult thing for the child when one of the parents becomes addicted to something, but it is even more difficult and confusing when both parents are enslaved and absent. In a situation like this, the child is left feeling abandoned and confused. Get to know your child/children so that you will recognize signs of depression. Depression is a serious condition and should be taken very seriously. Not everyone, especially children, can recognize depression, and many people don't know how to deal with it.

Depression in children is treatable but often unrecognizable because parents think that the child is just going through a rough time. Children who have a hard time concentrating, having an increased or decreased appetite, is sleepless or sleeps excessively, is irritable or angry, continuously feels hopeless, unworthy, or sad, and withdraws socially may be suffering from depression and speaking with a healthcare professional should be a top priority. These symptoms differ in children, and may not all occur at the same time. Please be aware of your children and what they feel, and ask them how different experiences make them feel. If unrecognized and untreated, depression can deepen and lead to disruptive behaviors, addictions, or even suicide.

# SAFE, YET INSECURE

One day near the middle of the school year, I decided to try and get my mind off of things. I loved to run, so I got permission from my grandma and joined the track team. I found genuine pleasure in thinking of all of my problems and leaving them at the start line, running my way to freedom, and I felt as though once I reached the finish line that my problems were still behind and, for a brief moment, that they hadn't followed me. I was also a part of the chorus and the marching band, so that took my mind off of everything that was happening at home. Sports and music were a great relief for me and gave me a positive way to release my anger. It wasn't a cure all, but it took my mind off of things for a while. Twin and I had a key to get into the house, and most of the time when we got home, Grandma was still at work and Mommy was nowhere to be found. So we'd let ourselves in, and we'd worked together to get our homework done and our clothes ready for the next day. Well, we tried to work together. Twin never wanted to do her homework, and then she would fake like she didn't know how to do it, so I had to be the mother figure and make her do it. And when Grandma would get home, we would sometimes have time to play cards, a game or two of one of our favorite board games, Trouble and UNO. Then we'd be called by Grandma to eat dinner and get washed up for bed.

We were pretty much on our own for most of the day, and for a very short time, I thought that it was pretty cool that there were no parents around telling us what to do, but I quickly realized that I wanted rules and boundaries. I felt like no one loved us because there were no rules or boundaries. When there are no rules or boundaries, it seems like no one cares what you do or what happens to you. As a parent, I set boundaries and create rules because I don't want my child to be hurt, be disappointed, mistreated, or dead. I want to teach her right from wrong and what is healthy and what is not so that she can be watchful of certain situations and people.

It was so sad and unfortunate that after the bullying during the day at school, there was no one home when we got there to tell us that things would be okay. We were in sixth grade and would soon be going to junior high school, but we still felt lost, and although it wasn't major to some, going to junior high was a big deal.

Our elementary-class trip had just been presented to the class. We had the grand opportunity to go to Orlando, Florida, and enjoy Walt Disney World. Now as soon as the trip was mentioned, I knew at the back of my mind that we would not be going, so I immediately began to formulate reasons why we didn't want to go so that I could try and defend me and Twin against the bullies. My heart was overjoyed for a brief moment when the trip was announced but quickly sank to the soles of my feet once I realized that we probably wouldn't be going. The truth was that we wanted to go badly!

I went home and told Grandma and eventually told Mommy, and at the back of my mind, I thought that we had the chance to go. One day, Mommy came home from a long absence. We were sitting at the table eating, and I knew that when she walked in the door, she wasn't going to give us a hug or anything. I had become so hardened by this time in my life, and I still didn't see any light at the end of that dark and lonely tunnel. I don't know if this next statement will make sense, but because I knew that Mommy wouldn't hug us, my hopes weren't up, but still they were up. And just as I predicted, she walked right in and said a simple "Hey." We sang in unison, just as we'd done in the past, "Heeeeey, Mommy."

The first thing that Grandma said was, "Liz, where have you been? I'm tired of having to raise your kids while you run the streets for days at a time, and these girls need their mother."

I wanted to jump up and high-five Grandma and give her a hearty "Hurrah" and "Yeah, that's right" or "You tell her, Grandma." But the only part that stuck with me was when Grandma said that she was tired of raising us. The first thing that I thought was, *If Grandma is tired, then who's left to take care of us?* I had just begun to work out how I was going to beg and plead with Grandma not to stop loving us and raising us.

We used to sleep in Grandma's bed sometimes, and after we bathed, we did something that we had to do before Grandma would let us climb into her bed, and that was to brush our feet off and then brush all of the "grit" out of the bed. Grandma hated to lie on her bed and feel anything that didn't belong. She didn't want to feel dust, dirt, or anything that felt gritty. And to this day, I just have to brush my bed out and my feet off before I lie down in my bed. So after we completed our task, we happily jumped into the bed and snuggled up against our grandma. Although I could see that she was tired, she always welcomed her twins anywhere she was or went to.

Just before I dozed off I looked up at Grandma and pleaded, "Grandma, can you please keep loving us?"

Grandma seemed genuinely sincere, and there was one thing that she always said, which was,"Awwwww, bless your heart." She followed that up with, "Of course, I will always love y'all." And that gave me a boldness and peace to stand up against any bully at school and anyone else outside of school. I went to sleep with a smile on my face and I slept better that night than I had ever slept since I could remember. It meant the world to me to hear that someone actually loved me, and even if the kids at school constantly called me and Twin "ugly, black, skinny, crackhead kids, and poor," for the first time in my life, I *didn't believe it*!

I grew more and more excited about the class trip. And one weekend, my daddy showed up and wanted to see us so that he could buy us some Easter shoes and an Easter outfit, and somehow, he and Mommy began to argue again. Now when I last saw my daddy, he was filthy, incoherent and didn't recognize me or my twin and grandmother. But when he showed up this time, he was polished and dressed nicely and the familiar smell of his aftershave filled my nostrils and brought back memories of happier times. I was ecstatic when my daddy walked up and although we were too big for him to scoop us up as he did before, we ran to his side and latched on to his waist and had planned to never let him out of our sight again. We never asked where he had been or why he had come back into our lives at this point, but all that we cared about was that he was back. I didn't fully understand how they hadn't seen each other in such a long time, or so I thought, and when they did, they still found a way to just argue and cuss at each other. And of course, Twin and I were the main discussion. I constantly heard Mommy telling Daddy, "You don't do nothing for my daughters," and Daddy constantly replying, "You don't let me, and you keep my daughters away from me."

It was so frustrating because weren't we both of their daughters? And is that the reason that we hadn't seen Daddy because Mommy wouldn't let us? Now that I was a little older, things were becoming clearer to me. One of the constant questions that kept me awake at night was, *Who is telling the truth?* Although neither of my parents ever sat me and Twin down to explain things or to talk about anything, they constantly argued about us.

Things had also gotten a little more complicated in school. T, the bully, had something new to bring to everyone else's attention.

In her mind and opinion, she just knew that we wouldn't be going on the class trip because our parents were absent and we didn't have the money. Although I totally agreed with her, I didn't want it broadcast to everyone in school. But little did she know, my daddy was working on it, and I overheard him say he would be going with us. That was a little different for me because although he was our daddy and we adored him to no end, I felt like I really didn't know him. So I didn't know how the trip would turn out. The last time that I saw him, he didn't even know who I was, and this created a little barrier between us. Nevertheless, he was my daddy, and I loved him no matter what he did, and I loved mommy just the same.

I had always wondered if Mommy felt the same way about Daddy. Did she still love him even though they constantly argued? Did she ever love him at all? She had always said so many mean and hurtful things about Daddy while we were in her presence that I didn't know how she felt about him. She constantly said things like, "Your father ain't worth nothing. He don't care nothing about neither one of y'all." She called him names like "black, sorry, worthless, stupid, and ugly," just to name a few.

Up until this point, I had never heard Daddy say one negative thing about Mommy. He would always ask us, "How is your mother doing?" Although he was frustrated with her and her actions and they argued and cussed at each other when he was in her presence, he had never said one bad thing about her to us. One day at school, I raised my hand to go to the restroom, and Mrs. Barino granted my request. On my way back to the classroom, the bully decided that she had to go to the restroom too. She looked me square in the face and asked, "Who did your hair?"

I dryly replied, "My mother." I didn't want to give this girl any fuel, and I surely didn't have the desire to hold a conversation with her.

As I continued my journey back to the classroom, she said, "Oh, its pretty."

Because I wasn't in my happy place, and I knew that this wasn't sincere, I didn't even give her any eye contact, but I replied, "Thank you," and I kept moving. Just the other day, she had called me so many names because I didn't have new clothes on and I didn't have a so-called status like she did. I was truly fed up with her and anyone associated with her. I was tired of the sleepless nights and the pain that I felt from all of her verbal attacks and being followed home daily with those stupid little songs that she made up.

Well, I guess she didn't appreciate me not looking at her in the eye and not bowing down to her anymore. And when she followed us home, I didn't even give her the satisfaction of acknowledging her presence. I didn't hear a word that ever came out of her mouth, and her little entourage just sickened me.

I didn't know how I was going to handle all of this, but what I did know was that I was absolutely positively about to blow up. All of the feelings of unworthiness, anger, sadness, emotional pain, and loneliness that I felt were all built up, and I didn't know how to release them. But I quickly found out how I was going to release it.

One day after school, I stood outside to wait for Twin to come out. The bully was there too, and her sad little entourage obediently followed her. As we began our short trek home, the little entourage followed shortly behind us. Twin and I were also crossing guards, and as we stood on the corner with our bright-orange belts on, the bully and her small entourage stood there on the corner, singing and taunting us. They began singing one of their many songs, and this time, the bully picked up some small rocks and began to throw them at our heads.

Once we reached our front door, I walked Twin in the house, and I calmly placed my backpack down on the floor and headed back outside. I stood tall and looked the bully right in her face.

She obviously thought that it was quite funny because she began to laugh hysterically. Because for the very first time, I was very serious about letting her know that she would not be able to push me around for another moment. I didn't say anything until she stopped laughing and gave me her undivided attention.

She quickly stopped laughing and shoved me and said, "What you out here for? Acting like you gonna do something?'"

I still didn't feel like having a conversation with her, especially at this moment. She stepped closer in my personal space and shoved me a second time.

So I looked her straight in the eyes and told her, "I want you to stop following us home and to stop talking about us."

She still thought it was a joke, and for a third time, she shoved me.

I punched her square in the face and asked her entourage if they wanted some as well. Everyone stood with their mouths open, and I looked all of them up and down and walked off, backward, of course. I was prepared for the five of them to jump on me and beat me down, but as I calmly and slowly approached my door, I turned back and asked all of them again, "Do y'all want some too?"

No one was able to answer because the bully was standing there steaming and her entourage was now pointing and laughing at her. I wondered if she knew how it felt to be embarrassed and pointed and laughed at. And from that point on, I didn't have a single problem with the bully or anyone else for the remainder of the school year. I am not saying that violence was or is the answer to solving any problems, but she threw things at me and shoved me more than enough and not to mention the emotional torment that she had been putting me through for some years.

# *Life Lesson:*

People can only be pushed so far. Even children have feelings and thoughts. Some people are more patient and longsuffering than others, but there comes a time when we have to stand up for ourselves and not be anyone's doormat. Standing up for yourself can be done in many different ways. I think that it is always best to make a responsible adult aware of a situation where you are being assaulted, or bullied. Whether the assault is physical or verbal, some sort of authority should be made aware and ensure that the situation is documented. If the situation continues, then you have to be able to defend yourself. Do remember that even in defending yourself, there are consequences to any and every action.

# A STRANGER'S HOUSE

We started to get closer and closer to our class trip to Disney World, and I was so very excited to know that we could finally spend some time with Daddy. I was also hoping that he could get us some new clothes to take on the trip because the kids would probably continue to talk about the clothes that we had. I was so very excited that Daddy sometimes popped up at school to see us and paid for our trip in bulk payment, and I thought the world of him for doing that. And every time that he showed up, I made it my personal business to let all of the other kids know that my daddy was around and that he did care for me and that I was going to Disney World with the rest of them. Ever since I stood up to the bully, I was feeling more confident in myself, and I just wish that I would've had someone to talk to about it.

Mommy knew that Daddy was going to Disney World with us, and she seemed to be mad about it. We would try to go to her and talk about it because we were excited, but she would quickly shut us down and say, "Get out of my face because I don't wanna hear that." And she also said things that I didn't fully understand, like "Y'all think just because he's doing this one thing that he cares. He don't care nothing about y'all, and y'all are just as stupid for believing that he cares." I thought that it was an honorable thing that Daddy was trying to step up and do something good.

At least he recognized us, and he did take the time to hug us and surprise us, even if he wasn't a rich or perfect man.

Our trip was coming up in about two more weeks. One day, we were getting dressed to leave and go somewhere unknown with Mommy. Sometimes before she left, we would ask, "Mommy, where are you going and can we go?" And she'd *always* reply "No, y'all can't, and I'm going to see a man about a horse." I never understood what that meant, but I did know that seeing this man about this horse kept her away a lot and she never came back with this horse. I loved horses and was sorely disappointed that whenever she did return, there was no horse.

For years, I never considered that we had absolutely no way to feed or house a horse, but I needed something to believe in. After about ten years, I had another aha moment, and thought to myself, *Heeeeey, we're not getting a horse.* It was a personal sad day for me, but now I can look back and smile every time that I think about it. I often still bring it up to my mom, and we laugh together. Someday, I'd meet this mystery man and his horse and give him a piece of my mind because he was very rude and inconsiderate for keeping Mommy away from us so much and never sending her home with the horse. Mommy had us walking and walking and walking to the point where our feet burned.

On this particular day, we had caught a bus to Northeast, Washington, DC, to some unknown person's home. Once we got off of the bus, Mommy stopped at a corner store and bought us a juice and a bag of chips. Then we continued to walk some more. The bus ride seemed so short compared to all of the walking that we had done on that day. And we were very tired and were ready to see where we were going and to whom we were going to visit.

Once we arrived at this person's house, Mom walked us up to the third floor of this townhouse and sat us down in a room and told us not to move and that she would be downstairs. I remembered leaving Grandma's house at about 9 o'clock in the morning, and the time was now about 4 o'clock. I had to use the bathroom, so I cracked the door open and peeked into what was a narrow, dark, and dusty hallway. I wanted to obey Mommy, but I'd rather get a whoopin' for leaving the dingy room than for peeing on myself. I also learned at an early age to pick my battles. I called out to Mommy, but she didn't answer. I called out to her about four or five times, in hopes that she would answer back since I didn't know where the bathroom was in this stranger's house. I told Twin to come on and try to use the bathroom while I was going because I didn't know when Mommy was coming back. And as always, she was very reluctant to follow me, but she knew that I was not gonna leave her alone in this dim and spooky house.

Although it was broad daylight outside, the inside of this house was so dusty, gloomy, and dark that it reminded me of the high rise. None of the blinds were open, and every door that we walked pass was closed. So there was no other choice but to continue to call out to Mommy and start opening doors. The fact that Mommy wasn't answering was just plain scary, and Twin was now crying. I wanted to cry too, but I had to keep my eyes clear and open so that I could be ready for anything that could've come our way. I was trembling, and it didn't help that I had to pee. I and Twin were of the same height and weight, but I pulled her in closer to me so that I could protect her.

After opening three doors, I tried the fourth door, and thankfully, it was the bathroom. But I remember when Mommy would take us to different places, she would always tell us not to sit on anyone's toilet seat. She never explained why we shouldn't sit on the toilet seat, but as I grew older, I figured it out. We didn't know who lived in this house or if they had any disease. And she never had to remind me because once I realized that there were people that I didn't know, I wasn't going to sit on it anyway. She warned us that we wouldn't want any infections.

So I told Twin to go first, even though I didn't know if she actually had to go. But it was my duty to protect her and make sure that she was okay first. As she used the bathroom, I danced around and crossed my legs while trying to hold it all in. So after she had finished, I squatted quickly and relieved myself. And we went to wash our hands so that we could get out of this dingy bathroom. I really wasn't even comfortable pulling my panties down because of the dirt and stains all over the toilet, sink, walls, and window. I had become somewhat of a stickler for germs at a young age. It wasn't because of anything that anyone had told me, I just didn't like the fact that germs were on things and could possibly cause me to catch a cold, virus, or anything else that didn't make me feel good.

We crept back to the stuffy, dark little room that we were in before so that we could wait for Mommy to come back. I'm glad that we found the bathroom because Mommy was taking a long time to return. We were restless and getting hungry. Some hours had passed, and I wasn't sure how many, but what I did know was that it was dark now, and this room became even creepier than it was before. There was a bed, but I wasn't about to lay in it because I didn't know whose bed it was. I was sleepy, and so was Twin, so I had her lie on my legs while I sat on the floor with my back up against the bed frame.

I didn't know if I was asleep or awake, and I just knew that my head kept snapping back and forth and I had to occasionally readjust because my butt cheeks had fallen asleep. I woke Twin up because I had to stretch my legs and back. I constantly peeked out of the window to see if Mommy was among the commotion below on the street level. I looked at the little raggedy clock that was on a small black stand beside the bed, and it said one thirty-two.

This house was dark, and there was constant noise, but I didn't know where anyone was. The front door opened and closed more than fifty times, but Mommy still hadn't come upstairs to get us. Out of the many people that were walking back and forth past the front door, I couldn't see Mommy. Well, many of those strangers were beginning to enter the house, and although I wanted for one of them to be Mommy, no one came upstairs. We were starving, and the time was somewhere near four in the morning. We had fallen asleep again, and this time, the sun was peeking through the dingy curtain or blanket that had been tacked to the wall. I couldn't tell what it was that was hanging up at the window. I just knew that I had left the curtain open a little in great anticipation that Mommy would return.

It was now close to seven o'clock in the morning, and Mommy came strolling into the room with the same clothes on that she had left in. I had urinated on myself because I must've been in a deep sleep. My mommy was infuriated that I had wet my pants, but that was the least of my worries. I nervously reminded her that she had told us not to move, and I made her aware that we had gone to the restroom once before this little incident. I was so worried and scared of what had happened to Mommy, and I also constantly wondered if Twin was okay.

My twin was always my top priority, and I never had time to worry about myself because I wanted to make sure that she was okay. Many people always wondered how we were the same age but had totally different personalities. And I always believed that it was because I was a whopping eleven minutes older! That has always been my story, and I'm sticking to it! Since my twin was the more sensitive of the two, I felt a need to protect her. I never knew exactly how I was going to accomplish that, but I was willing to spend my life trying.

## *Life Lesson:*

Being left alone in some stranger's house was just another example of a time that we could've been abducted or abused. We were exposed to frightening situations occasionally, and a child has no way of just letting fear roll off of their backs and move on with life. Fear paralyzed me! Although it didn't paralyze me physically, it caused me to emotionally and mentally become still.

Because I was so consumed with each traumatic event that had occurred in my life through the sixth grade, it caused me to stop feeling. I felt a little freer when I stood up to the bully, but other traumatic events caused me to feel as if I was in bondage all over again. I felt trapped inside of a dark tunnel and couldn't seem to feel my way out. I didn't care about much anymore, and I went to the other end of the spectrum. At first, I wouldn't talk much or say anything about anything. But fear caused me to begin to lash out at people and say whatever I deemed appropriate. I didn't care how people received me or my words, and I had been overflowing with anger and resentment.

Parents should help their children to find a release. I am thankful that the afterschool activities that I did have the opportunity to participate in were there, because I honestly don't know how else I would've relieved some of the negativity and anger that had been built up for such a long time. Once your children reach a certain age, I firmly believe that it is okay for you to explain things to them. Instead of always telling them no, explain why something may be harmful to them. Explaining things give the children a clearer understanding of why they shouldn't try certain things and why they shouldn't be willing to accept certain things.

# REHAB OR RUNAWAY

Since I took on the job of protecting my twin, I surely had plenty of opportunities to do so. We were ten years of age when Mommy had become angrier. She'd have us to do chores around the house, and they never seemed to be done to her standards. Of course, we were young, so things weren't going to be done exactly as she wanted them to be done. We swept, wiped the tables, washed dishes, and kept our room somewhat clean. Twin was slightly more disorganized than I was, so I pretty much always had to "assist" her with her side of the room.

I truly dreamt of the day where I would have my own room because the fact that Twin didn't enjoy cleaning as much as I did was very frustrating. But I couldn't blame her. As much as she did clean right, Mommy never gave her the credit that was due her. Whenever Mommy was around, she would constantly disapprove anything that Twin was involved in. And Twin constantly wanted to prove herself. She would often do my chores just to see if Mommy would accept her. She was constantly hit and threatened simply because she looked like our father. And in my opinion, it was cruel because that was something that she had no control over. I think that Mommy knew that too, but Twin still had to pay the price for her genetic makeup.

I did wish I was ridiculed like Twin because I was someone's look-alike. It was a hard place to be in for me because I was always told, "Girl, I don't know where you came from,'cuz you just don't look like nobody." That caused me to feel more alone than ever before. At least Twin belonged and could identify with being associated with a family member. I honestly don't know which was the more harmful of the two: being slapped and despised because "You look just like your black, ugly, sorry, no good father" or because "You don't look like nobody in this family." I'm thirty-four years of age now, and I can still say that both statements probably hurt just the same.

I made a vow at the tender age of ten to be mindful of speaking badly about other people because you never know the hurt or pain that they are experiencing, nor do you know what kind of things they had to deal with when they aren't in your presence.

I cried more and more at night as I lay wide awake in my bed because, although I was surrounded by people, I felt so alone and unwanted. Although twin and I were extremely close, we were fighting separate battles, but the same war. We were constantly trying to earn the approval of someone, anyone.

Grandma was having more and more health challenges, so her condition seemed unstable, but she continued to be strong for us and show us that she loved us. It was so hard to see her laid up in a hospital and seeming so helpless. She was a strong, independent woman, so anything less than that was difficult to accept. Grandma was the glue that held the family together. She would always be sure to plan and host cookouts, Thanksgiving or Christmas dinners, and more. I often wondered if she weren't around, then who would be the one to get everyone together for holidays or a just-because cookout?

After one of Mom's "leaves of absence," she showed up knowing that Grandma and our uncles had been looking for her, which is why I believe that she tried her best to stay away. After about a week of looking and asking around for her, she showed up on a Saturday morning. We ran down the street to meet her halfway, and her response was, "Who been round here looking for me?" Then she answered her own question with, "I don't need nobody looking for me." So we ran back toward the house to tell Grandma that mommy was home.

As soon as Mom stomped through the front door, Grandma met her in the kitchen and said, "Liz where have you been?" Her reply was, "Mama I'm grown." We all knew that she was grown, but the fact of the matter was that she needed to be responsible. There was the mention of Mommy going to a rehab center, and she quickly dismissed that idea by screaming, "I don't need to go to no rehab. I don't have no problem." And then she quickly turned and jogged out of the front door. I, Twin, and grandma ran after her as Grandma yelled, "Liz come back here." People in the neighborhood were stopping and looking at us as Twin and I ran with tears running down our faces at the same time. All that I could think of was if Mommy was ever coming back. She was always so angry, and this time she was really angry.

For the first time in my life, I felt sorry for her. She looked pitiful. She had lost weight and didn't look alive. She was in total denial about her addiction, which meant that she wasn't going to be able to get help or help herself. She knew that she had to go away for a while, but I didn't think it was a big deal because she was always gone anyway. She later submitted and was enrolled in a drug-rehab program and was successful for a short while. I don't know what caused her to go back to using drugs, but she did.

Shortly after she returned from the rehabilitation program, she was working again and was gaining the weight back that she had lost. She seemed like my original mom again. She was smiling, happy, and calm. She was funny and was interested in what was going on around her, and she was interested in me and Twin. We missed her dearly, but although we were happy to see the 'original' Mom, we didn't know how to deal with it. We had become so accustomed to her screaming, cussing, yelling, and being mean to us that we couldn't enjoy the original her. We were still sorely afraid that she was going to snap and revert back to the addict at any time.

But as I stated earlier, I just learned to enjoy the good times whenever they occurred. Once I sat down, grabbed a dictionary, and looked up the word *addiction*, I had a better understanding of what it was. I understood that Mommy and Daddy had habits that they had a hard time controlling. I still didn't understand why they wanted to do drugs or what was so good that made them go back for more. One thing that I did know was that when I became an adult, I would not be the same. So I went back to what I knew best and what I was comfortable with, and that was being angry, for reasons that I couldn't even identify. There were so many reasons that I was angry but I didn't know how to clearly communicate them to anyone, and no one ever asked.

Whenever we had the chance to have some fun, we would hang out with our cousins, and we thoroughly enjoyed ourselves. We played freeze tag, tag, Mother, may I?, hide-and-seek, jump rope, and other games that we made up on the spot. As kids, we were never bored. My generation was so creative and active. By the time we were ten, Lil B was twelve, and Sparkle was seven months younger than we were. Lil B's first little brother was born in September 1988, and he was simply adorable. Lil B's mom, my aunt, was gone quite a bit too, and he had the responsibility of taking care of his younger brother at times. I never thought that it was fair to force a child to take care of another child and especially without any other parental guidance. Children already don't come with an instruction booklet, but parents had the instinct that children just didn't have.

Daddy was coming around every once in a while, but we gladly received him each time. We thought that some time was better than no time. We had it where sometimes, one of our favorite uncles—and we have five favorite uncles—would sneak us over our daddy's house, even if it were for a few minutes. We had brief moments occasionally to see our aunts, uncle, and cousins on our father's side. We always had a true blast whenever we were able to see them, and they always welcomed us. They told us that they loved us and wanted to spend more time with us. They would always tell us to ask our mother if we could come over more often. But we knew that she wouldn't allow us to. Mom was barely around, and she didn't know that we were visiting with them anyway. Just for the simple fact that they were related to Daddy, Mom wouldn't approve of it.

There was a time where we were in a school play. I got to play the role of a Dutch girl who wore these cool wooden clogs, and Twin got to play Raggedy Ann. We were ecstatic when Mommy came to the play, and she was very proud of us. One of the funny moments that we share today is the fact that Twin had this one famous line in the play, and when her turn came to say her one line, she did it loud and proud because she knew that Mommy was right there in the audience. When her part came, she stood tall and shouted, "New shoes!" For the first time since we were born and could remember, Mommy smiled and looked proud of us. Although our parts in the play weren't the major roles, we sure felt like it because Mommy was there. Daddy didn't make it to the play, but we were still satisfied.

We had been proud when we had finally made it to the sixth grade and were so ready to go and enjoy our class trip. Daddy promised us that he was going to attend the trip with us no matter what. So we hung on to his word. It was the day before we were scheduled to depart for the trip that the bully decided that she would try my patience. I thought that I had straightened her out once and for all, but occasionally she would throw some verbal jabs my way. And although each word that she said hurt me more and more, I never let her see it.

I don't know who came up with that stupid song, "Sticks and stone may break my bones, but words will never hurt me," because that was on the other end of the spectrum. That song was so far from the truth that I wish it had never been created. Words hurt dearly, and it had been those very hurtful words, whether they were true or not, that ripped my self-esteem and confidence apart daily. Words hurt, no matter when they are spoken. That may not make sense to some, but I'll be sure to explain myself on that later.

The bully and her antics were old, and now she had somehow recruited a couple of people to stand around and form a semicircle to make fun of me and Twin because she still thought we still weren't going to go on the class trip. She had lain low for a while, and I was enjoying every moment of it. I wanted so badly to stand up and shout to the whole school, *"My daddy has been paying, and we are going!"* But I didn't have the confidence to do so. Although

Daddy promised, he had promised many things before the class trip that never happened, and their teasing had caused me to doubt. He promised things like, "I'm gonna come around more, and I'm gonna buy y'all some new shoes, and I'm gonna make sure that I come and get y'all." But none of his promises were ever fulfilled. So again I found myself standing before the bully and her entourage defenseless. I just wasn't sure that what I was defending was worth fighting for.

It was early in the morning when they first approached me, and since I chose again to walk away from the situation, of course, they followed. They had a bad habit of spending so much of their time taunting and torturing other kids, and I always thought that there were far more constructive things to do with their time. I mean reading, drawing, sports, and music were just some of the things that they could do to make their lives and mine better. I hated spending so much of my time trying to ward them off and shoo them away like pesky little bugs. For a while, the bullying stopped.

But this particular morning, the entourage followed us to the cafeteria. As I placed my backpack on the bench, one of the girls walked up to me and decided to say that I looked stupid and that my outfit was horrible. I politely grabbed Twin's hand, and we walked toward the serving line. Well, again that wasn't a good-enough response to her, so she decided to place her hand on my shoulder and spin me back around toward her. I gently warned her and said, "You don't know what I know, so I would advise you to keep your funky hands to yourself."

She thought that was so hilarious, so she took that same hand that she spun me around with and then plucked me on my ear. Now although I was small, I had a newfound boldness within me. And one of my major pet peeves was for anyone to put their hands in or near my face. It was mainly because the first thing I thought of on people's hands was germs. I calmly took a step back and strongly slapped her across the right side of her face. Her eyes grew extremely wide, and she raised her hand to swing at me. And again, to her surprise, I stepped back and took a boxer stand and air-punched a couple of jabs her way. I could tell by the sheer horror on her face that she wasn't expecting this at all, and when she stepped closer, she was welcomed to the sweetest two piece that anyone had seen me dish out. She stumbled backward and expected someone to catch her, but the crowd that she thought was for her stepped back and parted like the Red Sea.

Again, I'm not sharing this to condone violence. This is simply to advise all of the bullies out there that it is not okay to intimidate others and continuously badger and pick on those that you feel are smaller or weaker than yourself because you don't know when, what, or how they may step up and put you down. Instead of looking big, bad, and courageous, the bully really ends up looking like a wimp. Just because you are hurting doesn't mean that you have to make others hurt just as much or more than you are. It's important to deal with issues and anger and get some help from someone who is willing to listen and assist in your healing. I do believe that in some way, and at some point in our lives, we reap what we've sown.

## *Life Lesson:*

What goes around definitely comes around! Be mindful of what you say to people and how you treat them because you will definitely receive what you give. It may not be from the same person in the same day, month, or year, but I'm a firm believer that at some point in your life, you experience what you've dished out.

For those of you who are reading this and are hurting, talk to someone. It is not a weakness to acknowledge pain, but it is a sign of strength because you can't change things that you don't acknowledge. Parents should keep their word when they tell their children that they are going to do something. Children are expected to give honor and respect to their parents, and parents should be expected to build trust with their children by telling them the truth and keeping their promises. It is so disappointing when a child looks forward to that new toy or going to the mall and the parent never shows up or when the child reminds the parent of their promise and the parent acts as if they never said anything.

I can remember being disappointed over and over again. My parents would promise to reward me as long as I did good in school, and I did great. But the rewards never showed up. I was constantly promised new toys, clothes, and a host of other things that I never received. The broken promises caused me to have little faith in my parents' words. I had faith that they were able to make those things happen, but I had little faith in their spoken promises to me. Parents, build trust with your children and keep your word! The world will bring them enough heartache, lies, cheating, and bad experiences, and when you don't have a place of safe refuge at home, then you don't have confidence that anything will work out.

# DISASTER AT DISNEY

I had been bullied so much that it was definitely physically and emotionally exhausting. I got tired of the kids continuously talking bad about my hair, clothes, body shape, looks, and home situation. In all that we choose to do on a daily basis, there are decisions to be made and consequences for every decision, whether good or bad. This was a concept that no one taught me officially, but I learned it, and I learned it quickly. Since I was such a thinker, I would always ponder upon my decisions, and I made it a habit of thinking before I acted or reacted. That can sometimes be a bad thing because I tend to overthink things and think myself out of the right decision.

Our class trip had finally arrived, and just as we'd hoped, Daddy arrived too. We were sitting on the bus, and Mommy was giving Mrs. Barino some tips that she thought would benefit me on the trip. I overheard her whispering, "And make sure that Kita wears her bra because she don't like to. And make sure that she wears shorts because she always wants to be stuck in a pair of pants." I did not like when Mommy was gone, but at that particular moment, I was too embarrassed and wanted her to exit the bus so that we could leave and begin to get to know Daddy better.

There was some thirty minutes or so before we were scheduled to leave, and Mommy and Daddy started arguing. I wanted to climb under the seat and shrink away. I was so ready to leave Washington, DC, at that moment. And I heard Mommy say, "You better be lucky I'm not going, and I don't trust you with my daughters for a whole week." And Daddy replied, "Well, you ain't pay nothin' for this trip, so you ain't gotta worry about that." I didn't have a single clue as to how Mommy pulled it off, but somehow, she walked across the street and came back with her luggage.

As I saw her walking back across the street toward the bus, I immediately felt heaviness on my heart and tears in my eyes. I just knew at that moment that the trip would be a complete disaster. I didn't feel this way because Mommy was going, but because both of my parents would be in the same space. And whenever that happened, there was absolutely no joy in the room. But Twin was ecstatic because she had a thought that maybe they would get back together and get married and we could be a real family. Although I desired the same deep down in my heart, I didn't feel like it would ever happen. It was extremely hard for me to even fathom the two of them reconciling. I honestly didn't even recall if my parents ever had an actual relationship where they loved or even respected each other. Well, I know of at least one time they did! They argued, cussed, and screamed at each other every single time they were in each other's presence. It was tiresome because no matter what they were arguing about, we were always the topic of discussion, and it seemed as though their anger was because we were born. They constantly put us in the middle, but we never had the chance to shed any light on the situation. I was the master at staying in a child's place, but if I had the chance, I would've asked both of them, "Why did you all have us?" If we were the cause of that much pain and anguish, then why were we born? I spent a lot of time wondering why I was born.

We boarded the bus, and one of us sat with Mommy and the other one with Daddy. I was so clueless at that time because if Mommy didn't have money to pay for the trip, I was wondering how she would have money to spend or pay for food and anything else that required money. I never understood why I was so consumed with adult problems and concerns. I didn't have the complete responsibility of solving my dilemmas, but I felt as if I was forced into adult situations, and I was forced to be concerned with adult issues.

My daddy was a fun and playful man. He was like a big kid in a man's body, and at the time, I and twin thought that was so very cool. We laughed at Daddy as we rode the bus, and he made silly faces and did silly things. Every time a smile crossed our faces, Mommy looked at Daddy and rolled her eyes so hard that at one point I was afraid that they would roll out of her head. When we'd arrive at a rest stop and exited the bus to stretch, we'd ask Daddy to walk us to the snack machine or to the front of the restroom. But Mommy was sure to let him know that just because he paid for the trip, it didn't mean that he was the primary caretaker. I wanted so badly to remind her that it didn't seem as though she was the primary caretaker either.

All of the kids would turn and stare or point and laugh every time that my parents would get into an argument. I was almost ready to say that I would much rather have been teased for not being able to go than to have them arguing for the entire trip. The morale continued to go south, as the bus traveled south. Once we arrived at the hotel, it was dark, and we checked into our rooms and rested up comfortably for the night. I and twin stayed in a room with Mommy while Daddy got a separate room. I totally understood why! I had wished that Twin and I could've gotten a totally separate room for the two of us, on Mars. I wanted to be so far away from the stressful and disgruntled parents.

Most children who were in the sixth grade expressed how they desired new bikes, Adidas, Etonics, BK (British Knights), or some Guess jeans. But there were two things that I desired at the ripe young age of eleven, and that was peace and direction. The sad thing was that I didn't see either of those two things in my near future.

The next morning, we got out of bed, washed up, and got dressed. The previous night was one of the roughest nights of sleep that I had in a while. I tossed and turned because I heard those horrible echoes in my ears all night; those stupid songs that the bully and her backup would repeat tormented me all night. I had a nightmare where the kids followed me to Disney and followed me around and tormented me with their words the entire trip. I heard their voices as I rode all of the roller coasters, and at every attraction that I stood in line for, they were there and singing and taunting me.

I had gotten to the point where most days, I couldn't even look in the mirror because even though I didn't want to admit it or believe what the other kids said about me, I did believe it. And when I looked in the mirror, I saw a skinny, black, ugly, stupid, and poor girl. My heart knew that it wasn't true, but my head didn't agree. I lost so much sleep, and I only wished that I had the courage to not believe those things. I wanted to stand up to all of the mean kids, but I didn't have anyone to back me up. So my self-esteem continued to shrink away, but I was determined to fight back. I didn't know how I would fight back, but I put all of the negative emotions into my school work and continued to stay on the honor roll. I never missed the honor roll, yet I still felt like I was the stupidest kid on planet Earth.

We left the hotel in hopes that we would be able to just enjoy the day while we got on all of the rides. We had to ride the rides with an adult, so we'd switch parents after every couple of rides. Mommy and Daddy continued to argue between rides. So after one very heated argument about nothing, Daddy got so mad that he literally ran off and hopped over a fence to get away from Mommy and her harsh words. When he jumped the fence, something went wrong, and he fell and landed hard on his arm and broke it. He had to be rushed to the hospital and had to have a cast put on it and a sling to hold it up. So of course, after that, he wasn't very happy.

And just like always, they continued to argue, and Twin and I continued to suffer the consequences. Because of their constant bickering, Daddy took it out on us and refused to buy us any souvenirs. And yet again, there was more fuel for the kids to tease us with. He knew that Mommy couldn't afford to buy us anything, and so he used us as a way to get back at her, just like the time that he took our food from us at the table and dumped it down the garbage disposal. We didn't enjoy any more of the rides for the remainder of the trip because of what was going on between our parents. So that was truly a waste of our precious time, and I would rather have missed out on that trip. But things were what they were.

# *Life Lesson:*

It has always been my belief that if the two parents don't get along, then the children suffer. I didn't want to live in a two parent household because of the way that my parents were to each other. I personally would rather have one stable parent rather than two unstable parents. Some people believe that the parents should stay together "just for the kids." But in my opinion, that is sometimes more unhealthy than one strong parent raising the children. Whatever it takes to create a healthy and peaceful environment, then that is what should be done so that the children can feel safe and enjoy life.

Parents should not take their anger and frustration out on their children, and they shouldn't constantly be the topic of conversation during heated arguments. A child should not have to hear their names come out of their parents' mouth when they are arguing about something. It causes the children to believe that they are the problem and it is their fault that they were born.

# CONFIDENCE BOOST OR BUST

We returned from the trip and were anxious to graduate from elementary school and to move on to bigger and better things, like Hart Junior High School. We were just ready to move on with life. We had high hopes that things would get better soon.

As always, we were the talk of the school and how our parents fought the entire time that we were in Disney World. Mommy made sure that she reminded us of how stupid we were for believing that our trip was going to be a success, and she reminded of how our father had failed as a father. She spoke about him so badly that we didn't even know if he truly loved us or not, whether he wanted us or not. And of course, after that Disney trip, he was missing in action for months.

I never understood why Mommy called me stupid so much, when I was always on the honor roll. I even went to the National Spelling Bee. I had won the spelling bee at my school, but when I got to the finals, I was too afraid and I lacked confidence that I backed out once I got there. Mommy was so upset at me, and as badly as I wanted to compete, I was too afraid that if I didn't win that people would think that I was really stupid. Mommy was infuriated, and she pulled me to the side and encouraged me (or the lack thereof). She pulled me close and grabbed me by the ear, like she use to do when we were in public and being disobedient. She calmly said, "You have done all of this to get to this point, and you need to get your little scared butt on that stage. You done dragged me all the way here for nothing? Stop acting so doggon' stupid."

Well, needless to say that didn't help me at all. I cried and cried and refused to go onto that stage. Besides, Mommy already thought that I was stupid anyway, so what was the point?

My teachers believed in me, but I needed for my mommy to believe in me. That just seemed totally impossible because nothing that I and Twin did was good enough for her. Neither Mommy nor Daddy had ever told us that they loved us or believed in us. Family members on my father's side told us that they loved us, and that meant a lot. But a child needs to hear it from their parents. We had the pressure of fighting bullies off during school, and our second battle was fighting for acceptance at home. We wanted to do any and everything just as long as Mommy or Daddy said that they were proud of us or that they loved us.

I knew that there was a great chance that I would have won a top spot at the spelling bee, but I was just too frightened. So we left the spelling bee, and I felt totally defeated. I had felt defeated on a regular day, and I was constantly afraid of my parents being more disappointed in me and them not liking me more. So I felt like no matter what I did, they would still argue and cuss and fight about me and Twin.

We finally made it to our sixth-grade graduation. It was a joyous day because we were so very excited to be going to seventh grade. We were hoping that things would be a lot better in junior high school. We had the pleasure of going over our uncle and aunt's house during the summer, and we were able to go to summer camp and have some fun times.

But that time seemed so short. The summer passed quickly, and we were preparing for the big seventh grade. We hadn't seen Mommy much over the summer, just about the same amount of time we would've seen her if we were home. We were hoping that we could go school shopping and get some new clothes for seventh grade. We didn't know how or from whom, but we had hopes. Our bodies were going through so many changes, and we didn't know how to deal with it or what to expect. It was an important time in our lives, and I wanted to ask Mommy some questions about the changes and the feelings that I was feeling. But of course, that was just another dream. There was nothing steady or consistent in my life, and I was so very angry about it.

We had started seventh grade and had to get used to switching classes. Unfortunately, we attended school with the same people that we went to elementary school with, and I was not looking forward to more years of torture from them. Junior high school was bigger, and although we saw a lot of familiar faces, there were plenty of unfamiliar faces as well. We did not go school shopping so that we could get new clothes, and of course, we wore what we had. I was so angry about everything, and so I went into seventh grade just upset and uninterested.

Life seemed so hard, and I needed help with school work, but I had to make sure that Twin was taken care of. My twin was, and still is, awesome! We were always very close and had never been separated. We were starting to look different, and our clothes didn't have to be labeled any longer. Twin developed much faster than I did. She had started her period near the beginning of seventh grade, and she had begun to develop, whereas I was still in line, waiting patiently. In elementary school, we looked just alike. We were the exact same size and all, and we definitely used that to our advantage. Since our general interests were different, and always had been, we may have had the opportunity to switch classes unnoticed. I'm just saying!

Although we are identical twins, we didn't look as much alike as we used to. We always had to battle with people in junior high because they insisted that we were fraternal twins just because I was taller and thinner and Twin had developed before I did. I had also grown taller, whereas she didn't. They never understood that identical twins meant that the two babies shared a sac, whereas fraternal twins' sac split into two separate sacs. I was so tired of constantly hearing the kids at school teasing me and saying "You are so skinny" and "Your twin looks better than you." I'd have to go home and hear "You are too skinny" and "You're just as dumb as your no-good father."

I never imagined that life could be so exhausting and people could be so discouraging. Everyone made it seem as though being thin was some sort of disease. I ate and ate and ate, except when I was sad because my parents were gone. I did have a high metabolism, and I couldn't help that I didn't gain weight. I had such low self-esteem, and I would never look people in the eye. I'd always sit and walk with such a hump in my back because I was convinced that people wouldn't see me if I hunched down or avoided making eye contact. I automatically thought that everyone felt the same about me, and when they saw me, the first thing that they saw was a skinny, black, stupid girl.

About halfway into the seventh-grade school year, I began to have a little trouble in school. I enjoyed learning and was always eager to learn, and because I was lacking sleep, I was having trouble paying attention in class. I began to have a little trouble in my English class, and I had a big test that was coming up. After Mom wasn't seen for about four or five days, she finally showed up at the house. It was two days before my test, so I went to the bedroom where she was lying on the bed and asked her if she could help me to figure out whatever it was that I was having a problem with. She replied, "How am I gonna help you with something? This is your work, and you're the one in school, not me." So I was left to figure it out all on my own again.

One of the most frustrating things was that I didn't have a mom who was willing to help me, listen to me, teach me, and lead me. I felt as if I was wandering aimlessly around some foreign planet and I didn't know where I was going, how I had gotten there, and why I was there. By the time I was eleven years of age, I had spent so much energy trying to figure everything out. I had to figure out how to take care of another child, keep up with my school and homework, and protect the both of us from dangers that were beyond my age. Grandma was sick on and off, and we had the responsibility of caring for her as well.

I was so angry because I didn't feel like I was prepared to take on all of the pressure, and I didn't know how to overcome or deal with it. I had developed such a horrible attitude and had begun to lash out at any and everybody. I was only eleven, but I was cursing a lot, and I was very mean. I felt like I had to get at people before they hurt me and I had to snap at them before they said something about my physical appearance or life. I was hurting, and the only way that I knew how to release that hurt was to let the world know that I was hurting. I held way more emotions inside than I let out, but for all of the times that the bullies had picked on me, I had some emotions stored deep inside of me.

I was the type of person who wouldn't just come right out and be nasty to someone. But whenever someone would ask me a question, I would do what I thought was right at the time and "tell it like it is." I didn't have the slightest regard for anyone else's feelings, whether they knew me or not. And I thought that it felt good to let off some steam. I had mastered the art of sarcasm, and it felt good when I went flying off of the handle, at least I thought it did. I was so deceived.

My god brothers taught me to fight back physically, and my uncles taught me to fight back verbally. The first time that my mom caught me cussing on the elementary-school playground, she whooped me on the spot. But I didn't think that it was fair because my uncle had taught me everything that I knew. I was initially exposed to vulgar language by my mom, but when she said it, it sounded so mean I didn't want to repeat it. But my uncle made it sound so fun. He would always cuss with a smile.

See, in my family, when they sat around and told stories that we children weren't supposed to be listening to, cussing was a natural and normal part of life. But my mom, aunts, and uncles didn't cuss in front of my grandmother and their elders. That was just a normal rule that my family had. They found it extremely disrespectful to cuss in front of the mothers, aunts, uncles, etc. But boy, when the elders left the room, it was on! And the children who were eavesdropping in the next room were rolling on the floor laughing.

In case you all don't remember, Mom gave me permission to cuss one time. And later when someone brand new came along and said one thing to me, I let all of the previous cuss words out that I had all bottled up inside. I thought it would make me feel better, and even before the whoopin', I felt horrible for stooping as low as I did.

# *Life Lesson:*

It is the parent's responsibility to teach the children valuable lessons and they should be a good example for the children to follow. It doesn't make any sense to teach a child not to do something that they constantly see their parents do. Children are always watching and listening, even when you don't think that they are. Parents should always encourage their children to overcome obstacles and build up their self-esteem when they feel like they can't accomplish something. Deep down in my heart I know that I could've won that National Spelling Bee because I was very good. But because I didn't have any positive words from my parents echoing in my head and any encouraging speeches from my parents in my heart, I felt like I couldn't do it. When I stepped up on that stage and went toward my chair, all that I had to rely on to calm my nerves was negative words that had been planted for so many years. They were the same words that kept me awake at night, and that kept me from concentrating in school. They were the very same words that caused me to walk with my head down, not looking people in the eye when I spoke to them and to just feel all around bad about myself. Parents, be sure to reverse any negativity that your child may experience outside of the walls of your home. Speak positively to your children, on purpose! Even if you don't believe in them, make sure that they feel like you do. Your children should feel like they are the most valuable, beautiful, intelligent people that you know.

# OPTIMISTIC

During most of my life up until this point, I had spent it being unhappy and hurting. I had experienced more fear, hurt, and anger before I became a teenager. I was in desperate need of love and was having a hard time finding it. I thought that as I got older, I would find peace and happiness. But it still seemed so far away. I was afraid to get any angrier than I already was because I just felt like I was going to explode.

The most fearful moment in my life was one day, when we were about eight or nine years of age and I, Twin, and Mom were walking home from Grandma's house. We lived on Brandywine St. and had just walked down the hill when there was crowd standing in the middle of the street. Two individuals were arguing intensely, and Twin and I grabbed Mommy's arms because we were more afraid the closer that we walked toward the crowd. Mommy shook us loose from her arms and said, "Stop being so scared and come on here," as we continued to approach the angry men in the middle of the crowd.

Just as we had gotten about fifteen feet away from the crowd, they quickly scattered, and I wondered why. Just as quickly as the crowd had scattered, one of the angry men in the middle pulled out a gun. They exchanged a few more words, and the man without the gun was shot in the face at point-blank range. I was horrified and had wanted to stop in my tracks, but Mom kept on moving around the man lying in the middle of the street and continued on. Later on that day, Mom overheard Twin and I talking about the situation and threatened that we shouldn't speak another word about it or else.

By far, it had been the most traumatic thing that I had encountered in my time on the earth. And for months, I was afraid to go outside. I knew that dangerous people with guns were out and about in the middle of the night but never had I imagined that this type of incident could occur in broad daylight. It was a bright, sunny, and beautiful day!

I continuously thought that life was way too difficult. There were a few good times, but how was one person or child able to handle so much pressure? The adults didn't even seem to have so much fear and stress in their lives. They went about their day having fun, while their children were off learning life on their own. I just didn't understand how adults were comfortable with this.

I was thirteen years of age in the seventh grade, and junior high school wasn't as much fun as I thought it would be. It was definitely better than elementary school by far. I had learned to focus on my studies a lot better, but it still was a little rough. Mom and Dad were still absent from our lives, and Grandma was sick on and off, more on than off. A lot of the people from elementary school went to the same junior high school that we attended, and some of the kids still picked on us and talked about our looks and our clothes. It didn't hurt any less, but I was so much stronger than I was before. But I really think that I was just angrier. A lot of things hurt me, but I made it a point to act as if nothing surprised or hurt me, and that was the only way that I felt safe.

The only way that I knew how to deal with things was to act as if I didn't care. I forced myself to believe that if I acted as if I didn't care, the sadness and hurt would just go away. I constantly had my defenses up, and the anger was just a result of the sadness and hurt. The broken promises also played a big part in my lack of trust for people.

When I and Twin turned thirteen, our physical appearance changed dramatically. Twin had developed much faster than me, and as her curves began to appear I became even angrier because I was left out. But I did grow taller. So there was another challenge to face. Although Mommy constantly said that twin looked just like her "ugly black father," people always saw it fit to remind me that she looked better than me. People were cruel and senseless enough to just walk right up to me during lunch and say, "Why are you so ugly and your twin so cute?"

It was always so surprising to me that one human being could be so mean and hurtful to another human being who had done absolutely nothing to harm them. I had gotten into the habit of walking with my head down and not looking people in the eye because I didn't want anyone to get a glimpse of the pain that I was experiencing. And even more than that, I didn't want anyone to see the lack of self-esteem that I had. My family members never failed to comment on how "straight up and down" I was, and I don't know if they meant any harm, but they sure did some harm.

I still managed to make it through the seventh grade and was in the eighth grade now. There was one time in particular when Twin and I were having a program at school and we wanted Mommy to come. But we hadn't seen her for a little over a week. We only had a couple more weeks before we were moving on to high school, and we were so very excited. We weren't excited at the fact that a new experience was ahead of us but that we were a little closer to being able to leave the house and be on our own. Twin and I often spoke of and intricately planned out our wedding day and what our lives would be like once we were out on our own.

Well, our program had come and was now gone. It was one of the best experiences ever because a musical group called the Sounds of Blackness came to our school and performed. And

I'm sure I would've enjoyed the program a whole lot more if I hadn't been so sad. Every song that they sang was supposed to be inspiring and uplifting, but all that I could do was sit in the very last row of the auditorium and cry until I couldn't cry anymore that day. Every single song made me think of my parents and how much I missed them and how much they were missing. But in the midst of my sobbing, there was one song that woke my aching heart up and it's a song that I live by to this day. The Sounds of

Blackness performed this song titled, "Optimistic" and it seemed to give me some hope that it was still possible that I could win and rise above all of the anger, sadness, pain and resentment that I was harboring.

My parents had two of the best daughters that they could've been given. We were mature, obedient, and had wanted to do well. We didn't have a lot of supervision, but we did right on purpose and simply because we wanted to. I just wanted someone to hug me and tell me that everything would be all right. I thought of all the cruel things that the kids at school said and how no one was there when I got home.

A couple of days after the program, a couple of the kids were standing around at lunch and saw me walk by, and a couple of them had to make it their business to tell me that they had seen my mom at one of the popular drug spots on Wahler Place. It was a spot that people in the neighborhood commonly referred to as the other side of Wahler Place because it was on the opposite side of "the hill." And again I couldn't defend her because that may very well have been true. I couldn't prove or disprove that statement. I had spent so many years, up until this point, where I had to make up a reason that she wasn't there, no matter how stupid my reasons were. I had been in so many physical and verbal altercations while trying to protect me and Twin, and I was tired. Now back to a couple of days after the program, my mom decided to show up. She was filthy, her breath was horrible, and her hair looked like she had a creepy nightmare and she tried to yank it out of her head but never tried to straighten her hair back. Half of it was matted to her head, and the other half stood tall and pointed in many different directions. Her clothes were wrinkled, and she smelled as if she hadn't showered in at least two weeks. This wasn't the first time that we had seen her like this after she had been on one of her hiatuses, and I feared it wasn't the last.

None of that bothered me as much as it had before, and what bothered me the most was that she showed up at our junior high school looking like that. When we received the call to come downstairs from our classes with our belongings, we had no idea what to expect. When we entered the front office, there she stood. Normally I longed for a hug, kiss, or some form of affection from her. But this time, all I could do was cry and hold my head down. And for the very first time, I didn't want a hug or anything from her. I was extremely embarrassed and angry. I longed for her and Daddy's acceptance, but I was so angry that I didn't even want it. What I wanted was a normal life. I wanted for my parents not to be drug addicts and to support us and come to our school programs and tell us that they loved us and wanted us. I wanted her not to show up looking and smelling the way that she did. It was by far the most embarrassing thing that had happened to me. It was even more embarrassing than the cafeteria whooping.

I don't think that Mommy and Daddy had an idea of how much we had to deal with daily because of them.

# *Life Lesson:*

It is never the best option to hold so much anger inside. If at all possible, find someone that you can speak to and that can help you to understand and resolve your issues. Most times, children end up acting out in many different ways, and it's not because they want to, but its because they don't know how to heal themselves of the hurt, anger, resentment, or just plain frustration that they feel. Children don't always know how to express themselves and even into their teenage years, they have a hard time getting adults to listen to them and understand the temptation and pressure that they face.

Children want to be accepted by their parents, and they seek approval in different ways. Sometimes children and teenagers do things to get the attention of their parents because they know that is the only attention that they will get. From a young age, children desire and require a lot of attention, instruction, and affection, and when they lack those things, they tend to act out. The child's/ teenagers attitude begins to change which in turn causes their actions to change.

Parents should give their children the attention that they need. This attention includes listening to them, uninterrupted and talking about anything. When you talk to you children about anything, then eventually you will be able to talk about everything. This type of open relation between parents and children should be welcomed, with boundaries, at a young age. It is then that a child feels safe and comfortable to talk to their parents and not hold so much aggression in.

# MOMENTARY STABILITY

After we had rebounded from the sudden shock of her appearance, we were ready to leave the premises immediately. But shock number 2 came shortly afterwards. We didn't get the opportunity to leave immediately because Mom told us to clean out our lockers because we were moving. We weren't too shocked because we often moved from our own apartments back to Grandma's house. So we weren't really nervous about that because we loved living with Grandma.

Well, we had briefly gotten excited and had begun to skip toward our lockers when I stopped in my tracks because it didn't make sense. So I turned toward Mom and asked her, "If we're moving with Grandma, why do we need to clean out our lockers?" Mom looked at me and said, "You did not hear me say that we were moving with your grandma—we're going to Maryland." We were sorely disappointed and didn't know how to process that news. Maryland wasn't far away at all, but we hadn't had any notice. At this point, we only had a short time before we would be going to the ninth grade. Although we would soon be thrust into a brand-new environment where no one knew us, the idea seemed ludicrous. We only had a few more weeks before we were to be promoted to the ninth grade. But just like anything else, we didn't have any say so in the matter. We hadn't seen Mom, and suddenly she shows up and just snatches away what we knew. We didn't like it at all. I was so nervous and had so many questions, and the main question that I had was, why were we just up and moving and especially to some suburb in Maryland? I was not a happy camper and was not in the mood for any more surprises. Although there were so many thoughts running through my head at this point, the only thought that mattered was that *I was going to miss my best friend*. Beside my favorite friend Tamara from elementary school, there was an additional favorite friend that I had. Her name was Nettie and both Twin and I really loved her and would miss her. She was witty, funny, smart and always available and easy to talk to. We walked the halls of our school together, walked the playground together and genuinely enjoyed one another's company. And at this point in time, she was one of the major concerns. Another thing was that we were going to be skipped to the tenth grade if we had waited another two weeks in the public school system in Washington, DC. But, again we didn't have any say-so in the matter and had to go anyway. We did make my mom aware of the fact that we were eligible to be advanced to the tenth grade, and we were told that we were moving at that time and that there should be no more questions asked or statements made.

One of the more constant things in my mommy's life was a family friend who I had guessed was her boyfriend. His name was Kenny, and we absolutely adored him. He was no replacement for our daddy, but he was the next best man. He was hilarious, kind, and he genuinely cared for my mommy. He cared for us as well, and he knew the whole family. He was always concerned about us, and we later found that he and Mom were moving in together and that was the reason we were moving to Maryland.

Maryland was just a matter of thirty minutes or so away, but the whole point was that we'd have to meet new people and adjust to a new neighborhood. But knowing that Kenny would be a consistent person in our lives was amazing and gave us new hope. He also wanted a better life for my mom and wanted her to clean herself up and be accountable and take care of her responsibilities, which were me and twin.

I had never approved of any of my mother's male friends until Kenny came along. I hadn't spent much time around him at this point, but one thing that I knew was that when he looked at my mom, he cared for her deeply, and I could see it on his face. And that was something that I couldn't even see in my dad. I felt a tremendous amount of relief and security with Kenny around because he actually cared. He cared about how me and twin felt and how we did in school. He was there to make us smile, and he actually sat down and listened to us. He also calmed Mommy down when she was getting rowdy, and when she would go on one of her mean streaks, he would always make her laugh and help her to see things from our point of view.

Kenny proved that he was in it for the long haul when I got into some big trouble at school when the principal grabbed my arm really tight because I entered the gymnasium with food in my mouth. We were not allowed to eat in the gym, and I knew that. But I had the remainder of my food in my mouth and was attempting to swallow it when the short little principal snatched me up so quickly that I didn't even know what to do. So my reflexes caused me to react. Unfortunately, that reaction got me suspended from school. But since the principal had handled me roughly, Kenny and Mom came up to the school and spoke with the principal, and my suspension was rescinded.

So we were prepared for our move, and about two weeks after the incident, we had gone to New Carrollton, Maryland, to see our new condo. I, Twin, Kenny, and Mom went to Aerhart Dr. to view what would be our new home. At first, I thought that it was very weird. Even the street names were weird. In DC, we had streets like Eighth St., Ninth St., etc. Because I looked so deeply into things, the weird street names meant that things in Maryland would be more complicated.

But once we arrived at the condo and found out that it was a three bedroom with a nice-sized balcony and nice playground in a grassy area, it was impressive. Having a three bedroom meant that for the very first time, I and twin would have our own rooms. That was yet another amazing discovery. So I and twin went and sat on the balcony to explore our new neighborhood. Mom and Kenny were in their new room while we chilled out on the balcony. About ten minutes later, Mom began to dance around the living room as if there was a big bug on her. She mumbled something incoherent and began to walk out of the door. So Twin and I followed behind her. She then exited the front door of the building and walked down the sidewalk to the main road and began to take her clothes off. We followed her and attempted to snap her out of whatever she was going through by calling her name out loud over and over again. But that was in vain because she continued to jerk her body around and look around as if someone was after her.

By the time she reached the main street, she was down to her panties, and just as she reached to take those off, Kenny ran and scooped her up off of her feet and quickly carried her up the three flights of stairs and into the condo. We were frightened as we had never seen her behave that way. We were crying and continually asking her, "Mommy, are you okay?" and "Mommy, what's wrong?" After an hour or so, she came down off of whatever high she was on and went right back to normal, whatever normal was. She acted as if an hour before she hadn't run through the street mostly naked.

From that day forward, she never mentioned it. She never again brought it up, and when we asked her about it, she acted as if she didn't have the slightest clue about what we were talking about. It was quite baffling, and I was clueless as to why Mommy was acting that way or why she had become so outrageous. We later discovered that she had smoked some "bad drugs." The term *bad drugs* didn't make any sense to me whatsoever because all drugs were bad.

When we moved to New Carrollton, Maryland, in Prince George's County, it was a strikingly different experience. The neighborhood was quiet, the grass was clean and green, and it took some getting used to. Not that my neighborhood in DC was a horrible place, it was just different in the suburbs. There was no one sitting on the stoops in front of the buildings, there were no gunshots or sirens during the night, and the condo was big and spacious.

I had only wished that all of the kids that had made fun of us could've seen it. I felt as though I finally had something to show off and something to call mine. Like the popular television show *The Jeffersons*, I felt like we had moved on up to the deluxe apartment in the sky. I felt worthy, and I felt like people would respect me more, although I wasn't paying a single bill, or so I thought.

After we had said good-bye to Grandma and moved all of our belongings into the condo, Twin and I set up our room rules. We had rules for each other as far as when we could enter the rooms, what could be touched and what couldn't, how long we would be allowed to stay in the rooms, and most importantly, there were to be absolutely positively no sleepovers! After all, we had experienced the sharing a room life long enough. Despite all of our rules, we stayed in each other's rooms constantly, and we were super excited to be able to nicely kick one another out whenever we wanted to.

The first week or two after we moved in and got settled, Mom was around quite a bit. She was still moody and fussing about every little thing, especially with Twin. And it was still because she looked like Daddy. Mommy would constantly remind us of her dislike for Daddy by saying, "I can't stand his stupid, black, trifling," blah blah blah. Her list went on and on, and sometimes I thought that she made up words that weren't even in the dictionary just to make him look bad. She always reminded us of how he'd abandoned us and how he didn't want anything to do with us.

For the longest time, I wanted to tell her that whenever she felt like it, she did the same thing that he did. They both suffered from the same addiction, but she attempted to make herself look and seem so much better than Daddy was. And I always had mixed feelings because I believed her sometimes and sometimes I knew that she was just being spiteful and ornery. But I never knew if what she was saying was actually true. So the only thing that was left for me to do beside wonder about the truth was to allow the anger to build up more and more. I couldn't say anything for fear of being told that I wasn't "staying in a child's place" or for fear of getting a whoopin'.

Daddy wasn't around to defend himself, so I didn't have a choice but to believe the things that Mommy would say, and I began to develop dislike and resentment toward my dad. I didn't love him any less, and I didn't favor or love Mom more, so I never understood what her point was and why she felt the need to put Daddy down in front of any and everybody.

Even though Kenny didn't know my daddy, it seemed as though he was taking up for him. We'd hear Kenny tell Mommy quite often not to bad-mouth our father to us or in front of us. We overheard him one night, saying, "Liz, can't you see the hurt on those girls faces when you talk about their father like that?"

And not so surprisingly, she replied "Don't you see the hurt on my face because I'm left to deal with the two of them and I have to look at them every day?"

I was appalled because she didn't deal with us every day, and it made sense to me that if you didn't want to deal with your children, then why did you have them in the first place? The question was always in my mind, and I'd constantly ask to no one in particular, "Why am I here?"

Kenny would shake his head and tell her that she was wrong. And then she'd get mad at him and storm off and slam a door or whatever it was that she touched.

# *Life Lesson:*

Change is good! And even though as a child we were taught that children don't have a say so in what happens in the house and what decisions are being made, I do believe that children should be sat down and made aware of major changes. When children have a certain routine and are used to certain things, making sudden changes can be very disruptive to a child's emotional well-being.

Having someone in the home that shows that they care about the child's well-being and actively listens to a child makes a big difference. It reduces negative stress and a lot of frustration. Children respond more positively when they feel as if their opinions matter and that they are important. Whenever my mom was around and wasn't high on some sort of drugs, she was amazing. She was attentive, funny, and just a wonderful person to be around.

# MORE RESPONSIBILITY

We were close to finishing the eighth grade, and it felt good to accomplish something. Knowledge is something that no one can take away from you, and each time I finished an assignment, I got a small amount of satisfaction. I thoroughly enjoyed learning and felt as if I could go anywhere in the world just by opening up a book.

One thing that I had always loved about school, was that after passing each assignment, homework assignment, test, quiz, and class I feel a sense of accomplishment, and I appreciated my education more. Each day, whether I attended school or not, I would sit down and curl up with a book and learn something new. I could go anywhere in the world and learn about any animal, plant, planet, or organism that I wanted to learn about. The world was fascinating to me and was filled with so many things and people, and I wanted to soak in as much of it as I could.

I had a strong desire to be a police officer when I reached adulthood, and I figured that if I couldn't accomplish that, being a lawyer would be my second choice. I was fascinated with laws and cleaning up the world by ridding it of the drug dealers who fed people like my mommy and daddy whatever it was that kept them smelling bad and losing weight and abandoning their children.

But my dreams were just that—dreams. They were desires that seemed to be out of my reach. I didn't know how I would become what I wanted. I had always had wonderful grades, but I felt like the dumbest girl in the world because Mommy had said so.

I felt like other human beings didn't even want to look at me because I was hideous and skinny. I liked boys, but I felt undesirable and unworthy of even one look from someone of the opposite sex. So I always walked around with my head hanging down and more consumed with thoughts of who was thinking the worst thought about me. And when people did attempt to associate with me, I never let them get very close because I thought that there was some ulterior motive. I would never let anyone see my smile because Mommy always said, "Wipe that stupid smile off of your face," and so I thought that it was just that. Whenever I did laugh, which was few and far between, I never forgot to put my hand or hands over my mouth so that no one else would have the chance to see that "stupid smile."

I wouldn't wear skirts because family members and strangers alike would refer to my legs as "table legs" and always reminded that I was slim by saying, "Girl, you are straight up and down," or "When you gonna get some meat on those bones?" I felt so disgusted with myself over things that I couldn't change.

Twin had it even worse. Mommy always found a reason to hit her or belittle her because she reminded her of Daddy. Mommy didn't care who was around when she would call us names or whoop us for something minute.

One time, when we were about eight or nine years of age, my aunt got into an argument with Mommy about something, and as I and Twin ran in front of Mommy to try and shield her from the verbal and almost physical attack, Auntie shouted, "You don't need to worry about me and my kids. Worry about your ugly little twins. Don't be jealous because I made cute kids and you can't seem to make none."

So we had constantly been on the receiving end of insults, and we hadn't done any harm to anyone. By the age of thirteen, we had been weary of trying to defend ourselves against family members and bullies. But we vowed to always stick together and take care of each other. And to this very day, we've done just that. Back to New Carrollton, we had been transferred from DC Public Schools (Hart Junior High) to Prince George's County public schools (Kenmore Middle School) in Landover, Maryland, to finish out the couple of weeks that were left to finish eighth grade.

It was 1993, and we boarded the school bus for the first time in our lives and were ready to finish out the school year.

It was another difficult transition because people looked at us as if we were from planet Mars. We got our class schedules and tried to find our way around the school. One day, I accidentally bumped into a boy in the hallway while I was trying to find my class. And because I was always on the defense and ready to defend myself, I dropped my backpack and held both of my hands out and looked the stranger right in the eye and said, "What's the problem?" Then I felt so ashamed when he backed up a step and said, "Whoa, whoa, whoa, my fault." I quickly gathered my backpack from the floor and said "I'm sorry. I was just trying to find my class."

Thankfully, the boy wasn't looking for a fight, and he helped me. I turned to thank him once he had helped me get to where I needed to be, and I said, "My name is Lakita." He said, "I'm Earl, and I thought I was gonna have to call you Tyson," as in Mike Tyson. We laughed and went our separate ways. I saw Earl a few more times after the incident, but we just smiled and waved. I made it through the first day at the new school and hoped that it wouldn't be so bad after all.

When we boarded the school bus the next day, we couldn't share a seat and had to split up and sit beside someone else. So I sat beside an outgoing but nice brown-skinned girl. I was to too shy to introduce myself, but she wasn't. She said, "Hey, where did you come from?" I said, "From my mom." We both looked at each other and laughed, and she said, "Girl, you know what I mean!" I filled her in on the way to school. I told her that the other girl was my twin and that we had just moved from DC. She seemed very funny and nice. And from that day forward, we were really cool. We spoke, laughed, and had casual conversation.

One day, I was in the cafeteria and had just gotten my lunch tray, and as I sat down at a table by myself, another girl who was sitting with the nice girl I had met on the school bus that morning started talking about the clothes that I had on. So I let her go on and on. She was singing the theme song from the game show *Wheel of Fortune*. She kept singing, "I'm a wheel watcher,

I'm a wheel watcher," and it was because I had on a *Wheel of Fortune* t-shirt. No, I didn't like the game show that much, but my wardrobe was just as slim as I was and I did wear the shirt way more than I ever wanted to. But that was one of the things that I was used to dealing with. I was used to people talking about my clothes being too small, too short, or too big. They never fit just right to me or anyone else. But I didn't want everyone to remind me of it.

So I heard the girl say, "Watch this." She got up and put her garbage in the garbage can and walked past my chair, bumped it with her narrow little hip, and sang the song again. Well, I guess I didn't react the way that she wanted me to, or for whatever reason, she walked back past me toward the table she just left and took her elbow and jabbed it into my back and sang the song again. I never understood why people didn't accept my casual, calm and sometimes silent response to their ridicule. I always gave people the benefit of the doubt and tried to go my own way and mind my own business. I'd sometimes give a polite response or none at all, but they always came back for more. I was never a trouble maker and I wanted nothing more than for people to leave me alone and allow me to be who I was.

I calmly got up from the table, cleared it of the mess that I created, and walked over to the table where she was sitting. My bus buddy looked up at me and looked at the girl who had been taunting me. Since her back was turned, I didn't want to take a swing or jab at her with her back turned because that was cowardly and sneaky, so I aggressively said to her, "Ay, you got a problem with your hands?" When she turned around, I grabbed her by the front of her shirt, which is what we called jacking somebody up, and lifted her up out of her seat slightly and repeated my question to her. And to my surprise, she didn't have a single word to say. Needless to say, after that day, she never uttered another word to me.

People often assumed that because I was slim and didn't look confident, I was passive. And at times I was passive, but only because I chose to be. I wasn't a troublemaker, and I knew that because I was so angry inside that it was best that I remain calm and keep my mouth shut. Just to clarify for those who are reading this, I wasn't a confrontational young lady and because I was more on the quiet side and because I was slim people just assumed that they could do and say anything to me. I only fought when I had to, not because I wanted to.

It may have been about a week or so after that incident, that it was already time to graduate and move on to the ninth grade. We had to get special permission to attend Fairmont Heights High School, but Mommy got it done and submitted all of the proper documents. We had heard a lot of people talking about that school and were excited that we would have the chance to attend. In that short couple of weeks since we had been in Maryland, we had to readjust to everyday life, and Kenny had been a constant person in our lives. Mommy had been around more also, and whatever Kenny was doing, it was definitely working. She had been in better moods, and her mood swings weren't as harsh as they had been in the past. We simply adored him, and if we couldn't have our daddy around, we wanted him to be the man figure in our lives.

We also received another piece of shocking information that would change life as we knew it. Grandma had become ill and was coming to live with us. We weren't thrilled at the fact that she was ill or that we now had to share a room. But at least we could live with Grandma again. We had missed her so much for the time that we were away from her.

I can't say that I was happy to have to share a room with my twin again. I really enjoyed and loved her, and it was just that she wasn't the neatest person on earth. And for the record, I was! I liked for things to be in their proper place and neatly tucked away from anyone's view. Twin, on the other hand, was more liberal with her belongings. She felt as if they would be put away when and how she wanted them too, and it drove me bananas.

Kenny was so supportive and had been around since we lived on Brandywine St. in DC. We also had the responsibility of taking care of my little cousins. Lil B had to take care of one of his little brothers, and we had another of his little brothers. My family was awesome, and I loved my cousins a lot. While we were living on Brandywine St., Day-day was two years of age, and he was the little brother that we never had. He was so much fun, and we just adored him and his brother Tay. We invaded their personal space with so many hugs and kisses, and we just knew that when they got older, they would probably loathe public affection. Day-day lived in our household with us on Brandywine, and of course, since Mommy was gone most of the time, I was the one who was charged with bathing and feeding him most of the time. And this continued even when we moved to New Carrollton.

Grandma moved in, and Twin and I moved into the one of the bedrooms and divided the room in half. Anyone who had ever entered into our room knew whose side of the room they were on. Twin's was cluttered and unkempt, while my side was organized, but we somehow managed to coexist and make the best out of the situation. Grandma had some health issues and needed assistance with bathing, eating, doing her hair, and completing other tasks that she was no longer able to perform on her own.

We entered into our freshman year of high school, and we were trying to have a good time with all that was going on at home. By this time, I was fourteen. My little cousins were in and out of foster homes, and Mommy was fighting to get full custody of them. My aunt had four children with the first being born in 1977, the second in 1988, the third in 1990, and her beautiful only little girl in 1991. We loved them and sympathized with them because they were in sort of a similar situation with me and twin. Their parents were struggling with addictions, and they were often left to figure things out on their own. No matter how Grandma felt, when we were not living with her, whenever she was able to come and physically check on us, she never failed to do so. When she couldn't come to check on us personally, she'd send one of my uncles to make sure that we were okay. All of us adored our grandma and appreciated everything that she had ever done for us.

Although Mommy had her issues, and things were tough, she was determined to get custody of my cousins in order to keep them together. I thought that it was the second most honorable thing that Mommy had done. The first was not aborting me and my twin. She could've chosen not to give birth to one child, let alone two of us. But she kept us, and I was so grateful for that. Mom has told us the story quite a few times that she didn't even know that she was having twins. I know that I personally would've been shocked, and I don't know how I would've handled it.

The child-protection system had my cousins separated into different households and none of us were satisfied with that. In fact, I was extremely jealous and more resentful than ever because Mommy was fighting hard for them, but she had two children of her own that she didn't seem to care one iota about.

## *Life Lesson:*

Though you may not understand certain things in life, I have always believed in giving honor where honor was due. My mom is very deserving of honor because of the fact that she didn't abort my twin and me. Even though she didn't know that she was having twins until my twin's foot poked out eleven minutes after I had been birthed she toughed it out anyway. And the sheer shock of that could make some women feel as if they aren't able to raise two children at once and was probably more unbearable than I could ever imagine. Also, my mom made a promise to my aunt that she would make sure that my little cousins stayed together and with the family. Mom never had a problem working and she was truly a people person. She still is a person who enjoys working hard and enjoying the company of people. And though it was a struggle, and my mom could've done some things differently, I was very grateful that she kept her word and she fought long and hard so that my cousins could have a roof over their heads. Even through her struggles, she kept her word. I never expected for my parents to be perfect, but I did expect them to be better. I don't think that any parent is or will ever be the perfect parent. And as children grow into adulthood, I don't believe that they should expect them to be. Will Smith said it best in one of his songs, sometimes *Parents Just Don't Understand.* That statement includes parents not understanding how to overcome their own obstacles and how to raise their children.

# HEARTBROKEN AGAIN

Kenny was growing more and more frustrated with Mommy because she wasn't trying to do better. Mommy was constantly screaming and yelling at us when she was around, and she didn't like the fact that Kenny would tell her that she was wrong. He was a great provider, and he was very kind to us. He sometimes sat down and talked to us and just listened to what was on our minds and in our hearts. No one had ever done that for us before, and that's one reason that we absolutely loved him. I could tell that things weren't going as well as they were before because Kenny was very short with Mommy, and they didn't seem happy. His answers had become one-word answers, and they weren't as funny and giggly as they once were. Mommy was staying at home more when we had first moved to New Carrollton, but that changed faster than we thought that it would.

Life in our new condo had become similar to life in DC. We were always extremely low on food and we were trying to cope. We worked hard in school and wanted to join some extracurricular activities, but Mommy wouldn't let us. We figured it was because she wanted to run the streets while we stayed home and studied and took care of Grandma. We could never hang out with our friends at the movies or stay after school for anything. So things got harder. Mommy was still getting high, and she would often just wander around aimlessly with her eyes red and her speech slurred. When she was sober, I think she was angry because she wasn't high.

My ninth-grade school year was great, so we asked Mommy if we could get an afterschool job since we were doing well in school. At first she told us no but later changed her mind because of a little persuasion from Grandma. We really wanted to work because we wanted to spend the money on groceries for the house. If we had to be in the house all of the time, we wanted to be able to eat. Mommy agreed and told us that we had to bring home all of our money and show her what we had made from each paycheck. And we did just that.

A very short while later, the tension in the household had gotten so thick that it was scary. It was scary for me because I was afraid of losing Kenny, and I just didn't know what was next. I had grown weary of working after school and trying to maintain my good grades, but it was to the point where we had to work in order to keep food in the house and to get our personal items. Grandma was on a very fixed income, and I thought that all of us would end up starving.

Grandma needed help too. She needed help writing because of a stroke that she had; she needed help bathing and going to the restroom. It was a difficult task for us on so many levels. So in order to spend some quality time with her, I and Twin would sit in her room for hours watching daytime soap operas during the summer months that we were out of school. During the school year, she'd fill us in on what was happening.

We would get her out of bed, and Twin would comb and brush her long silky salt-and-pepper hair, and we'd help her to get dressed. We had to help her do everything because the stroke and triple bypass surgeries had limited her mobility. She needed help standing up so that she could walk with her walker, she needed her bedpan emptied and her diapers changed, and she sometimes had open wounds from surgeries and skin grafts that had to be tended to. She needed help with simple things like eating, turning over in her bed and using the bathroom.

Since Mommy was gone a lot, my twin and I had the task of caring for Grandma, and my three beautiful little cousins. I loved them dearly, but it was hard for someone my age to have so much responsibility. I got little sleep because there was always someone who needed something. Grandma had a cowbell that she would use to get our attention, and I absolutely hated that thing. But her voice wasn't as strong as it was before, so she had to use it. Sometimes that bell rang three to four times a night, and we had to wake up at all times of the night to do things, like giving Grandma her medicine, changing her diapers, or helping her get up to use the bathroom. She had a portable toilet in her room that was purchased with her hospital bed, and of course, after she had used the restroom, the toilet had to be emptied and cleaned. My body was tired, and I always felt exhausted. I was always sad and had these emotional lows that were downright scary, even to me. I just wanted to have a normal childhood and teenage life, but that still wasn't anywhere in sight.

Things didn't work so well with Kenny, and just as I had feared, he left. Of course, I wondered why he left and if we were to blame. I figured that five children and a sick grandmother wore him down as well. I had often wished that I could just up and leave too, but that was just a thought and could never have been my reality. Daddy left us too, and we felt as if it were out fault because we looked like him and because we were stupid, black, and ugly like him.

This particular situation was even more confusing because we didn't look like Kenny and he wasn't stupid, black, or ugly, so I didn't know what else it could've been. I couldn't eat or sleep well for weeks after he left. I wasn't in a relationship with him, but I loved him so much and was having a hard time making it without him. Since Grandma wasn't in the best of health, I felt like he was my rock and my backup. Mom was so angry and ornery that no one could enjoy her presence most of the time. But there were times where she wasn't so mean. There was a time when my grandma needed some items from the grocery store and my mom, twin and me walked to the store in the snow and ice and slid pretty much the whole way there and back. And once we made it back home, grandma wanted her soda immediately, and my mom had to inform her of all of the trouble that we had gone through to get that soda. We had a very good laugh about that situation. So there were definitely some times that we did share some good laughs.

I loved going to school to get away from it all, and I wanted to stay at school as much as possible. We had met more new friends, and I was to the point where I actually enjoyed getting up going to school and didn't want to miss a day, although I barely ate and slept and I cried constantly. There was never a break or a time to rest and have peace and quiet so that I could gather my thoughts. Finally, my grandma somehow persuaded Mommy to let us participate in an afterschool activity and ride the activity bus home from school. So I quickly and happily tried out for the basketball team. In elementary and junior high school, I was a part of the track and field team. But my passion was basketball. I went through the tryouts and made the team. So after a short time had passed, we had to travel to another school for our first scrimmage. We went to the scrimmage, and I scored eight points for the short time that I was in the game. I had never played on an actual basketball team, and it was truly exciting. I had grown up playing streetball at the courts in DC, and almost everywhere that I went, there was a basketball in my hand.

When the team returned to our school after the scrimmage, everyone's rides were showing up to take them home, but I didn't have anyone. It was a cool, dark night, and I began walking to the nearest bus stop by myself. I felt very uneasy, but I didn't have a choice. It was shortly after 9:00 p.m., and about halfway to the bus stop, I heard something behind me. I was horribly afraid but was scared to look back. I was on the main street, and I bent down and acted like I was tying my shoe and verified that there was someone behind me. He was a tall light-skinned black male with a black windbreaker and sweat pants on. When he broke out running, so did I. There were no questions asked, and thankfully, I outran him.

I began my escape by dropping my backpack during the chase, and I was sweating bullets. I was horrified, and I didn't have a phone to call anyone. Once I lost the stranger, I backtracked and found my backpack and paced and hoped that a bus would pull up soon. By this time, it was somewhere close to 9:30 p.m. About five minutes later, a bus approached, and I was relieved to have boarded it.

It took me all of forty more minutes to reach the bus stop in front of my apartment complex. The scarier trek was from the front of the complex to the last building at the back of the complex. I gave it all that was within me, and I ran as if that stranger was chasing me again and finally made it home safely. Once I arrived, my mom and family were so worried about me, so I told them exactly what happened. I just knew that this would be the last of my afterschool basketball days. My heart was even heavier now because basketball was my outlet and my passion. I enjoyed the game and it was one of the ways that I could clear my mind and get away for a while, just like when I read my books.

## *Life Lesson:*

Being forced to do something that you're not ready to do or that you simply don't want to do can definitely harden your heart. And although things get difficult and you don't know how it will work out or if the situation will end positively or negatively, its important to find some sort of positive outlet. I didn't know it or understand it at the time, but I later realized that although it was a bad situation for me, there was always a positive in any situation. I eventually figured that since I was doing well in school and the house was being maintained successfully, there was no one else at that time who was better suited for the task than I was.

I am not trying to put myself on a pedestal or toot my own horn. I am simply saying that if God hadn't used me to be the one to run the house and make sure that things got done when Mom wasn't able to do them, then who would've done it? My cousins would've been split up, and my grandma would've been shipped off to some nursing home and may not have been cared for properly. And although I didn't see it at the time, my mom did me a great service. It wasn't the way that I preferred, but she taught me how not to be because of how she was. She taught me to be responsible, nurturing, and independent through her being enslaved to drugs and being absent a lot of the time. And she did take the first step and bring everyone together under one roof.

# THE MAN COMES FIRST

Since Kenny was gone, I felt like the weight of the world was once again on my shoulders. But Mom had gotten another "friend" named James who lived in a neighborhood that was not far from our condo. And when she brought him to the condo in such short notice, it was hard to wrap my head around it. Here was this guy that we had never seen before, and he was starting to spend the night at our home. He never talked much, and he wasn't even interested in getting to know anyone in the house. He stayed in my mom's room the entire time he was there, which was all of the time. He used our water, ate our food, and made himself cozy whenever he felt like, and I wasn't the least bit happy about that. Mom would sometimes be in mid conversation with one of us when he'd call her from the back room and she'd go running. And when she did take off, we wouldn't see her for the rest of the day or for the next two to three days. Just like always, we'd be left to fend for ourselves, and that meant I was left to feed, bathe, clothe, dress, monitor, and entertain Grandma, and my cousins. I really enjoyed when my mommy was sober and attentive because she was such a great person in her natural state.

Again, I love my twin, cousins, and Grandma dearly, and the point of me sharing this is just to reiterate that it was a tough position to be in, being that I was a kid and wanted to experience life for myself. I was a talented child and teenager but couldn't let any of my gifts be nurtured because there was no time. I could sing, dance, play the keyboard and trombone, write poetry and songs, play basketball and run track, and march in the marching band. I had high hopes that I would be able to go to college and maybe spend some time finding myself and my passion and then maturing to where I could use it. But a lack of time and a deep sense of pure fear kept me from sharing any of my gifts and talents the way that I should have. I was so paralyzed with fear that I just didn't believe in myself anymore.

I joined the Junior Reserve Officers' Training Corp (JROTC) program at my high school and was absolutely loving being able to wear a uniform. Out of all of the extracurricular activities that I was involved in, JROTC was my favorite. I had the chance to march, drill, and become more disciplined in my life.

The JROTC helped me to cope better at home. It didn't cure my frustration, anger, and resentment, but it sure helped me to react a little better. I had a bad attitude, and although I held it in a lot, I knew that it was there and it wasn't getting any better. Everything irritated me, and I never showed it until I was in my room, away from everyone else. I had little to no patience, but only with things that were nonliving. For example, one day, I was sitting on my bed folding up some towels, and because the towel didn't look exactly how I imagined it would look after I folded it, I became enraged and I began to unfold everything else that was already folded and started just throwing things to the floor.

I didn't have any other way to release my anger, and every single moment of every day was a new chance to choose my reaction. Many times I would have it out when I was in the shower or in the middle of the night when everyone else was asleep. I would take a blanket, pillow, or anything that allowed me to squeeze it, throw it, or bend it until I thought that I felt better.

Everything was a choice, and I was pretty good at knowing and understanding consequences. I spent a lot of time thinking things through and I didn't want to take it out on my grandma, twin, or cousins because it wasn't their fault that we were thrust into this situation. And although I was angry with my mommy and daddy, I was taught to be respectful, and I did just what I was taught.

There were times that I wanted to be so disrespectful—and I did, but it was just in my head where no one could hear it and

I wouldn't be beaten for it. But in my head was even a dangerous place to be because I wasn't coping as well as I thought that I should have. I didn't know where to turn or what to do, and I realized that being disrespectful or taking it out on someone else would not make me feel any better. I didn't like the instructions that my mom gave me to clean the house and cook and help the kids with their work, but I was determined to be obedient anyway and hopefully conquer the anger and resentment later.

One of my favorite uncles had moved into the condo, and we had a pull out couch and a separate mattress for the kids and all of that was in the living room. He had started to take us to see my dad again. I wanted to see my aunts and cousins on my father's side, but I had so many mixed emotions and I had grown hard and weary, so I wasn't interested in seeing Daddy. I was more angry because I was hurting and no one was making the pain go away. Naturally, no one is happy about pain, and no one wants to walk around without hope and feeling like there is no help or healing in sight. Even though I still adored my daddy, I was so angry with him because he hadn't done anything about our living situation and our emotions. I wasn't sure that he knew how to fix it, but he sure was aware of it. He and Mom had been very inconsistent in our lives, and I disliked both of them for it.

Since Uncle was in the house with us, things just seemed even busier than they were before. I loved having him around, and he looked out for us well more than I could've imagined. He had always snuck behind my mom and kept us in touch with our daddy and our daddy's side of the family. Whenever we went to see them, we had the chance to see what normal life was really like. We didn't go hungry, and we had time to kick back and have fun with our cousins and just be kids. We could act as silly as we wanted to, we could play spades for hours and hours, and we could run outside like nobody's business. Each time was a great time, though they were few and far between.

Now back to this James guy who had stuck around for quite some time, and I didn't even know his last name. One thing that I did know about him was that he probably had bed sores because the bed was the only place that he knew of while he was in our house. Of course, I didn't like him because a real man would allow you to get to know him and would show another person some respect when they walked into the house. He was a sorry excuse for a man, and I wanted him to be gone.

I knew that you probably shouldn't compare one man to another, but Kenny had set the bar so high, and this James guy was nowhere near the bar. I didn't know what my mom saw in him and what she thought of herself to even settle for someone like him. I didn't know much about men and relationships because no one took the time to teach me, but common sense told me that I didn't want to end up with a guy who wanted to stay around the house and lie in bed most of the time. Whenever she would cook something, she would make a plate and take it back to him in her room.

He didn't contribute any money for anything, but one thing that he was good at was mooching off of us. I say *us* because I, Twin, and Grandma were giving Mom money to help with bills. It wasn't much because Grandma was on a fixed income from social security or something of that nature, and Twin and I were working all of the hours that we could work at Roy Rogers.

During this time in my life, my grandma was teaching me how to pay bills and balance a checkbook. It was so exciting because I got to spend more time with Grandma in her room and learn more life lessons. Once she was able to move around more, we helped her into her wheelchair, and all of us, except Mom, would sit with her on the balcony, or we would sit at the dining room table and put a puzzle together.

Since we couldn't go out with our friends, Mom would allow them to come over to the condo, but none of the boys could go into our room. So there were six of our very close friends, three of which were females who lived in the same building, who would come over and play cards or hang out with us. Since the girls lived in the same building that we did, it was easy for us to get together, and we had a great time whenever we did.

Although I was tasked with running a household at such a young age, I wasn't happy about it. But things were what they were.

# *Life Lesson:*

When we as human beings are angry, we tend to think irrationally. I've personally never met anyone who says when they were angry, "Let me go and give this person who has upset me a big, warm hug." So we must make positive decisions on purpose. There will always be numerous opportunities to make bad decisions, and it takes lifelong practice to become good at making positive decisions so that we enjoy positive consequences.

It is also important to understand that as human beings, we will make not so good decisions, and we must not hold anger and resentment in our hearts towards those who do. We must never forget where we came from and must understand that we are imperfect people who live in an imperfect world. We must also not expect more of a person than they can give. I was so disappointed over and over again because I expected two people (my parents) to do more than what they were able to do. I expected them to be responsible and to keep their word to us, but the reality was that they couldn't do that.

# TRUE FRIENDS

School was going great, and it kept my mind off of things for a while. I was doing well in JROTC and was in the marching band as well. Although I couldn't play basketball at school anymore, I was still practicing at home when Mom would let us go outside in the front of the building. I, Twin, and two of our best girlfriends were singers, so we formed our own unnamed singing group. We would sit on the steps at the end of the sidewalk and sing for a couple of hours sometimes. We all had things going on in our households, but when we were together, we sang, laughed, and had fun, and we even tried to avoid talking about our household issues.

Music had always been a major outlet for me. I had such a gift and at one point in time I felt as if I would someday be a famous singer. Singing soothed me, and at one point, I wrote music as well. I was able to freely express myself through songs, and to this day, I still enjoy music a great deal. There were so many songs that expressed how I felt, and when I heard them, I could pinpoint in my mind exactly where I was at the time that I first heard the song. Songs made me reminisce about many things. I absolutely loved to sing and to write.

Our friends who lived in the same building with us rode the bus to school together and home and were very good friends. I personally enjoyed my friends' company, and it was always great to be around them and to get their input and advice on certain situations.

School had finally become 100 percent enjoyable for me by the tenth grade. My grades were still as good as they had always been, and I still enjoyed studying just as much as I had before. Learning never got old to me, and neither did my being able to escape to anywhere in the world through a book or documentary. Since I couldn't go out and hang out, I'd keep some kind of book in front of me.

To help with my anger, sadness, frustration, and resentment, I would write poetry and keep them in a binder under my bed. I wrote about any and everything that crossed my mind, and although I knew it wouldn't cure my hurt, it was still good to get it out of my head momentarily. I was enjoying high school as much as I could, considering my home circumstances.

I was now having these feelings in my body and was curious about sex and boys, but there was no one that I felt comfortable talking about it to. I could've asked my friends, but I needed guidance from an experienced adult who can answer any questions that I had.

I had the biggest crush on one specific young man, and we had had a few classes together. I thought of him a lot, and I adored him. I sat in class and watched him work and read, and whenever I had the chance to talk to him, I did. I always smiled when I saw him, even if he didn't acknowledge me or know that I was in his sight. He was smart, handsome, and funny, and I wanted so badly to be his girlfriend. But I was not nearly confident enough to approach him about it. He was tall, slim, light skinned, and had braces and glasses.

I had two very best friends who would tease me about him quite a bit. I never even dreamed that he would see anything in me and would ever be interested in someone like me. But I kept thinking of him and dreaming that one day he might be interested in me. He was so fine, and he was one of the reasons that I was so eager to go to school each day.

The parents of one of our best friend's, Nate, would allow us over their house, and we'd go just to hang out. His mom had a business baking and decorating cakes, and they were the absolute best cakes ever! I wasn't one who liked sweets or cakes much, but her cakes were divine, and she made everything from scratch. The cake was always so moist, and the icing was made from scratch. Every time we went to visit, we'd leave with a health-food tip and some cake wrapped in foil. His parents talked with us and gave advice on how to be successful in life, and they welcomed us with open arms each time that we went over their house. There was always so much peace when we went over there.

Our friend had a little sister, whom we called Nat, who was adorable and never said more than two words. Although she hung out with us sometimes, she was very quiet and reserved. She and her brother were on the quiet side, and he'd sit back and just observe what was going on around him. Someone would tell a joke, and the rest of the group would literally bend over laughing, but when we looked up at him, he'd be standing there with the straightest face that I had ever seen. He wouldn't crack a smile, and for a long time, I thought that he was such a kill joy. Over time, he loosened up, and we all would just have a blast. I loved him so much and still do! He was the greatest brother ever. We referred to him as our brother and he was one of the best ones for the job.

Sam was another one of our very close friends and was the true clown of the group. We could always count on him to say something totally off the wall and irrelevant, and nobody ever took him seriously. He did funny impressions of people, and our favorite was his impression of an old drunk man. He'd stumble around and slur his words, and it made us laugh every time. He also made us laugh all the time when he sings the song "Hakuna Matata" from *The Lion King*.

Last but not the least was best friend Earl, who lived less than ten minutes away from our condo, and whenever we could, we'd all go to his house. His mom was always cleaning, and she never failed to feed us. I was always so happy to get some of her good home cooking. She never failed to put us to work either. It took us quite a few years to figure it out, but it was strange how we'd always end up at his house when a big cleaning project was going on. We'd scrub walls, sweep and mop floors, straighten up the basement, and dust. Amazingly enough, Earl would disappear every single time. And when the work was nearly finished, he'd show up again.

Earl and I were training together. He was on the football team, and I was in the marching band and JROTC; but I was still actively running track, so we would get together and exercise outside and fill a backpack with rocks and run with them on our backs. He was one of the guys who had a bunch of girls chasing after him.

One day, there was the normal bunch of us outside playing some game, and he pulled me aside to ask if we could "go together." Back in the day, we didn't use the word *date*, but when we liked someone, we asked if they wanted to go with us. Although I thought he was a handsome guy, I never thought of him in that manner because I didn't think that anyone would ever be interested in me. And why he was interested in me, I could not understand. But I was truly honored and flattered.

At first I thought that it was a joke, so I stood there looking at him in utter shock, and when he didn't say "Sike" or "Just kidding," I thought that he had lost his mind. But anyway, I thanked him for the gesture and told him that I wasn't his type of girl. I told him that I couldn't go out on any dates, and more importantly than that, I let him know I was a virgin and had planned on staying one. He looked shocked that I had told him no, and his reply was, "Well okay then." I asked him, "Can we be best friends then?" But I had already assumed that we were best friends anyway. So we settled that matter, hugged, and joined back up with the others. And from that day forward, he called me his little sister, and he treated me as such.

I didn't have to worry about a thing because Earl, Sam, and Nate had always looked out for me and Twin. They worked our nerves a lot because they were always telling us what to do, and I hadn't had anyone to do that in a long time. But they didn't care, because they kept doing it anyway.

My home girls were funny, outgoing, and loud. One of them didn't mind telling anyone what was on her mind, and everybody around us was going to hear about it. My Trinidadian home girl was sweet and laid back. She was honest, and she exemplified pure beauty. She had long shiny, silky black wavy hair that flowed down to the end of her back, and we loved to comb it. You'd often find her with all of her pearly whites showing. She showed her beautiful smile a lot and was constantly laughing about something. Another one of my girls was the Holly Robinson Peete look-alike. She was slim, had long hair, and was also loud and funny. Whenever she spoke, words came out of her mouth at about 70 mph and they had a New York twist. We often had to tell her to slow it down and run it by us again. We had so much fun when we were all together, and this group of friends brought great joy to my life because I spent so much time with them. I had one more very close friend, Jaime, who would always be there to talk to me and though we didn't live that close to one another and we didn't hang out after school as much as the other ladies, she was very special to me and I loved her dearly.

# *Life Lesson:*

There is great joy in surrounding yourself with true friends who love you and are willing to go through things with you. Friendships should never be one sided, and once you have found and surrounded yourself with good friends who deposit valuable ideas and vice versa, you should not let them go. Be sure to let your friends know how much you value and love them because once you grow up, you may never see them again.

My friends were a wonderful part of my life, and I honestly don't know how I would've made it through some of my toughest times without them. Friends don't put you in awkward positions where yours and their safety is compromised. They won't have you lying and covering for them, and they will have your interest at heart.

Parents should know who their children are hanging with. Just as my friends had a wonderful and positive impact on my life, sometimes it ends up being the opposite. Young people often don't know the real meaning of the word *friend*, and they often call people their friend well before the person has earned the title. The saying "Birds of a feather flock together" is definitely a true statement. If ever you wanted to know a person's character, you can always look at the people that they hang out with.

# THE END OF IT ALL

It was 1996, and things at home hadn't changed much. We were in the eleventh grade and were having a wonderful time at school. Grandma was struggling with her health, and Mom was still having issues with taking care of her responsibilities. She was still leaving and staying away, but each time that she left, she didn't stay away as long as she had before. She was so mean and unhappy and was always screaming and cussing at us for one reason or another, when she was high, and she was so demanding. Mom always wanted things her way or no way! She'd leave and tell us that we better have the house cleaned by the time she got back. We didn't know how long she would be gone.

Twin was always eager to impress Mom, so one day, she told me she'd take the day off and clean the house. Twin did a wonderful job, and the house was immaculate! I was really impressed with her, and I told her so, which boosted her confidence a lot. When Mom returned, Twin met her at the door and was so excited to tell her that she had cleaned the entire house all by herself. I had learned a long time ago that Mom's mood changed more than the direction of the wind. Whenever you are in her presence, there is no way to tell how she was feeling or what would upset her. Her mood changed so suddenly, and although her mood changed frequently, it was still shocking every time that it did.

Somewhere around this time, Mom had a new boyfriend named Randy. He was a very nice man, and we liked him. He was soft-spoken and seemed like a kind man. He also had two sons who visited with him often.

The one thing that I didn't like was that he and his boys stayed overnight, and that was two more children that I had to care for, although they were no problem, either. My twin and I double teamed a lot of the duties and made sure that the house was running as smoothly as it could've run. Randy's boys were kind and well-mannered little boys, and I had nothing against them. I was just exhausted, frustrated, weary, angry, and depressed. I was seventeen and didn't have any understanding of why I was the one who had to do so much for everyone else, and why I didn't have any say-so in anything or the power to control my world. I couldn't just tell Mom that I wasn't doing anything else for anyone because there was no one else to do it.

Grandma was frustrated because it was always so hard to get someone to come over and take her to her doctor's appointments, many of which were cancelled because of a lack of transportation and because she felt as if she was a burden to have to ask anyone to take her. I sometimes lay in my room and waited to see how many times Grandma would ring her bell for help and Mom wouldn't budge.

I had to wake up at six to go to school, stay awake in school, and maintain good grades, go to work after school, and return home a lot of the time to bathe and care for the kids and Grandma. I felt as though my life was at its lowest point, and there was only one way out.

Things were going well at school, and I was so depressed about my home situation that I couldn't see my way out. I slept only four hours or so a night, and I was absolutely worn out. But I was still an A/B student. I don't know how on earth I was able to maintain those wonderful grades while working after school and caring for four to six kids and Grandma. There was never any time to do what I wanted to do, which is why I did all that I could in school. I was still in the marching band and JROTC, and those were my absolute favorite groups to be a part of. I wanted to scream but was afraid that it wouldn't change anything, and no one would care anyway. I wanted to go to the movies, skating, to the mall, or anywhere to just get away from it all.

My grandma offered to pay for driver's education classes so that Twin and I could get a learner's permit, but mom wouldn't let us. She didn't give us any reason why we couldn't do it, and I guess we didn't need to know why. All that we do know is that we wouldn't be taking the classes and that is exactly what happened. We sadly, but quickly moved on from that dream. Grandma appreciated what Twin and I was doing for her, and she understood how hard it was for us, so she got us our own phone line in our room so that we could have a little bit of a normal teenage life. We were very grateful for everything that Grandma had done for us. I was also very grateful to have my friend's parents in my life. They were supportive and gave us great encouragement to continue to press on.

Everything was so hard, and one day I had had enough. I was tired of being tired. I didn't have any of the answers that I needed, and I was tired of not being able to find the answers. I was tired of being hungry and trying to scrape up enough food to eat and not knowing where the next meal was going to come from. We always had a hard time lifting Grandma up three flights of stairs while she sat on her wheelchair, and she was frustrated because we were frustrated.

Grandma was giving all of her money for bills, and I knew that because I was writing and mailing the checks. Twin and I were giving Mom our money to pay the bills, and we tried to keep a little money for ourselves, and a lot of the time, it disappeared during the night. There were a couple of times that I was awake and I heard someone come into our room and fumble around, and the next morning, the money that was in a hiding spot was gone. I pretended to be asleep, but most times, I was wide awake. I would lie awake and listen, and whoever it was would go in and out of the house a number of times during the night. I would hear doors opening and closing for hours throughout the night, and I often wondered how they expected anyone to rest with all of the commotion.

One day I was so fed up that I figured that I would show everyone that they would have to fend for themselves and that I was done losing sleep, time, energy, and money. I felt as if everything that I was doing was in vain and was unappreciated. I was tired of putting in so much effort and not receiving anything in return. So I finally figured it all out. One day after school, I sat down and planned out exactly how I would end it all. My final instructions and sentiments for my family were as follows:

*Dear family,*

*I have tried and tried to do the best that I could do with what I had. I have put all of my energy, time, money, love and dedication into you all. I know that I am no one's mother and I have never tried to be. I felt like I was forced into this adult role and I don't have anything against anyone. I am just tired and lonely. I am hurting more than I could ever express to you all.*

*I don't know what I'm doing or where*

*I'm going, but I feel like I'm just walking with blinders on. I want to be strong and I want to be there for everyone, but I just don't have the strength anymore. Please tell everyone that I love them and I'm sorry for letting them down. I'm so sorry if I have disappointed any of you. Just know that I did the best that I could.*

*This is no fault of your own and I just wish that I could've made things better. Hopefully, by the time this letter reaches your eyes you would have remembered me for who I wanted to be and not the tired, worn out person that I am. I just don't know what else to do.*

*Mom, all that I ever wanted was to know that you loved us and that you wanted us in your life. You and dad have been away from us more than you've been a part of us. It's very discouraging to see our friends living their lives and we just wanted the chance to hang out and laugh, go to the mall or movies and live a somewhat normal life. I do understand that it is an addiction that has the both of you away and acting the way that you are.*

*In case you didn't know, I wanted to tell you that it is not fair to force your child to grow up so quickly and take on all of your responsibility. As much as I love grandma, she is your mother, and as much as I love my little cousins and my twin, they are your niece, nephews and daughter that you birthed and adopted. So, I don't think that it is fair to have done all of this work for all of these years and never once did you hug me, kiss me or tell me thank you.*

*I don't even think that you love me and twin, or that you even wanted us to be born. Nevertheless, you had us and it would've been nice to act like you cared for us. As many times as you've called us black, ugly, stupid and dumb just like our father, you ripped a piece of us away every single time. Oh and another thing, words really do hurt! We've had to make excuses for you and daddy to the kids at school, and we've had to physically fight and emotionally battle on a daily basis because of you and daddy.*

*And it's been exhausting! Please show this to my daddy if you ever see him again. And for the record, he has never said one bad thing about you so I think that its best that you not put him down so much! Although you have never said it to me and twin, I'll say it on behalf of the both of us: I love you, despite what has been done or said. Please tell my grandma that I'm sorry that I couldn't do more for her and for all of the times that she had to ring that bell, it was bittersweet.*

*I despised hearing that thing, but I was overjoyed to be able to reciprocate the love that she has shown to all of us. I don't know what happens after death, like where I'll go or whatnot. But, I have to do something to relieve this anger, pressure, frustration, and this feeling of unworthiness. I was scared to go to a counselor at school to get some help because if you find out, you might beat me.*

*If you don't get anything out of this letter, please get this one thing! I forgive you, even though you may not think that you've done anything wrong. I have been practicing forgiveness for a long time, and I have learned that forgiveness is for me, not you. I forgive my daddy as well and if he ever has the chance to read this, please tell him that I'm sorry. I don't know what I'm sorry for, but I have always been sorry and always will be, mainly because that's what you said.*

*You have always told me "you'll always be sorry like your stupid father." And now, I believe you. One last thing, please know that you are no better than he is. Although both you and daddy are alive, I feel like you all left us a long time ago. As much as you put him down in front of any and everybody, you aren't doing any better than he is. Nevertheless, I've never loved either of you any less! Goodbye.*

I was so convinced that this was the only way out. I was tired, and I was ready to give up on everything. So I planned out specific details as to how I would take my own life. I was so frustrated that I figured that I would put everyone out of their misery. I had planned to carry out my mission while everyone else was asleep. After all, I was always up most of the night alone. I had ample time to do whatever I wanted to do because there was no supervisor.

My life had reached the point where it was just sad, and the night that I planned to make it all go away was the night that I was lying in bed and was waiting for everyone to fall asleep. I had planned to make it quick and easy, or so I thought. As I lay in bed with my eyes closed, I was almost at peace with my decision and plan. That was until I heard a voice say, "There's more." It crept me out horribly the first time that I heard it, and I hopped up out of the bed and began to search the house to see if some gentle intruder had entered. But I didn't hear any doors or anything open, so I shook myself and went to lay back in the bed.

About five minutes later, I heard it again, so I buried my head under the covers and hoped that what I had heard twice wasn't real. Close to twenty minutes later, when I returned to the surface, there was the voice again: "There's more."

I didn't know from whom this came or what it meant, but it put a complete stop to my plan. I eventually fell off to sleep and put my plan on the back burner. I didn't understand why I had this change of heart. And I can't say that it was a change of heart, but I just couldn't follow through with it at that time. I couldn't figure out what this saying, "There's more," meant. I was perplexed with questions, like "More what?" "More who?" "More when?" If it meant more heartache, more misery, more responsibility, more hunger, thirst or more things to figure out, then I certainly wasn't up for the challenge. Furthermore, I didn't even know who said it. Out of nowhere came this saying in this soft voice, and I didn't even know why I listened to it or why it chose me to talk to.

I was convinced that I was crazy and was ready to surrender to any authority so that they could strap me up in one of those white straitjackets. I simply didn't understand what was happening to me, and the one thing that I was sure of was that I was in such a sad state that I didn't know what to do and didn't care to do anything else about anything. There was one thing that I was sure of, and that was that I was an expert at hoping and wishing that things were different. I didn't have any faith in anyone or anything because all that I had experienced were disappointments and broken promises.

# *Life Lesson:*

I can only start by saying that there is absolutely no reason to take your own life. Even though things may seem to be horrible, as long as there is breath in your body, it is never too late for things to turn around for the better. Even though you might be afraid to seek help, it is better to go to a school counselor, friend, or family member for help.

There are many positive ways to release stress and tension, and bottling it up and holding everything in is not healthy. Even though you may not think that things will get better, have the slightest bit of hope that it will. Hope means that things may turn out for the best and that the things that you want can be had. It is always better to have hope than to focus on all of the issues and negativity in your life. I made the mistake of not talking to someone about my issues because I thought that they wouldn't understand and because I thought that my mom would punish me for it.

Find a way that is healthy and beneficial so that you can release stress and anger, because unhealthy thoughts often lead to unhealthy actions. There are many people who get into trouble with the law because of pent-up anger and negative thoughts that they end up acting on and doing things that harm themselves and others. Reaching out for help before making irrational decisions does not mean that one is weak, but it is a sign of strength and courage. Be free to express yourself tactfully and respectfully.

# MY FIRST LOVE

I had finally reached a point in my life where I knew that it was my time to make a change. It was 1996, and it was my senior year in high school. I was so excited because I just knew that Mom was going to give us more freedom and that she would realize that we would be graduating high school and moving on. I had a very strong desire to go to college or in the military. It had been a dream for me to finish school and go off to college, out of state, or sign up for the military so that I could go far away. I was hoping that we would be able to enjoy our senior year more than we had the previous school years. Daddy was still not present in our lives, and Mommy was still the same.

During our senior year, there were so many opportunities for us to get involved in some wonderful things at school. I had been promoted to the battalion commander in the JROTC program and the drill team commander on the unarmed exhibition- drill team.

My school life was so great, and I had a strong desire for my home life to be equally as great. But unfortunately, it wasn't. I had frequent thoughts of suicide, I was constantly sad while pretending that I wasn't, and I was uninterested and fatigued most of the time. I had learned so much over the years and didn't understand how I had made it to the twelfth grade. I was not clear at this point, but I had come a long way, and I thought that

I had seen the light at the end of the tunnel. With all that had happened in my life up to this point, I had many opportunities to lose my mind. In fact, I thought that I had actually lost my mind on a couple of occasions.

Twin and I had been out and were actively searching for an apartment to move into as soon as we graduated. We had already been working for most of our teenage life and felt like we were responsible enough to manage and finance our own household.

When Mom found out that we were looking to move out, she wasn't very happy about it. She didn't understand why we were so eager to leave. She didn't understand that we were seventeen years of age, virgins, making good grades, wonderful housekeepers and caretakers yet we couldn't have an opinion about anything, couldn't express ourselves, and didn't have full access to things in the house. So we really wanted to experience a different kind of lifestyle.

I was in a relationship with a guy who attended a different school, and he was my first serious relationship. I was deeply in love with him, and we spent hours and hours talking on the phone. He would come over to the condo to visit me, and we'd sometimes sit in the hallway of the building or outside and talk some more. My mom didn't like him, and she never gave me any specific reason. I had a couple of serious crushes on a couple of guys at my school, but I hadn't experienced love with a guy before. I thought of him day and night, and he made every effort to put a smile on my face.

Although we couldn't officially go out on a date, he never complained and was not ashamed to walk out in public with me. He never pressured me to give up my virginity, and he liked me for who I was. He understood my position at home and was still willing to stick around and support me. There wasn't a day that went by that we didn't talk, laugh, watch a TV show together while on the phone, and express our love for each other numerous times.

He made my life so much more bearable, and every time that I laid my eyes on him, I had a smile on my face. He was light skinned, with bright brown eyes that were close to being hazel in color. He always had a low and clean haircut, and he wore glasses. He was the first person my age who understood me. He never required me to give him anything, and he never pressured me for anything that I didn't want to do. In my opinion, he was genuine and sincere about his feelings toward me.

We spent a lot of time together. He would hug and kiss me, and I would enjoy every moment of it. I did not want to lose my virginity because that opened the door for a lot of things that I didn't want or need in my life, such as pregnancy or sexually transmitted diseases. I was one who was not ashamed of being a virgin in high school and was determined to remain that way because I didn't want to do what everyone else was doing and bring about unwanted problems. I didn't have high self-esteem, but I did value my body and didn't want to violate it.

My mom couldn't understand why I was in love and what I saw in him. The weirdest thing was when Mom and my uncle came home one day and saw me and my first love sitting on the steps in the hallway of the building, she ordered me to get into the house. So as she and Uncle walked up to our door, I gave him a big hug and a sweet and soft kiss, and we exchanged our usual "I love you," and then he left the building. Once I climbed the one flight of stairs and entered the condo of doom, Mom began to snap at me by saying, "So what, are you having sex too?"

This time, Uncle stepped in and said, "Even I can tell that these girls are not sexually active. All they do is go to school, work, come home, and take care of things round here."

My insides smiled so big and wide, and I wanted to run, jump, and hug Uncle because he said exactly what I was thinking. I wanted to tell Mom that I wasn't even interested in losing my virginity and that I had goals and things to accomplish. Not that I wasn't curious, because I was oh so curious. I was increasingly curious when my love would wrap his arms around me, hold my hand as we walked down the street, or kiss me. I hated to be apart from him and whenever he departed, it saddened me.

Mom got close up to my face and angrily asked, "How can you be in love with someone that you're not having sex with?"

I simply replied, "Easy."

She seemed to always believe the worst in us, and she always thought that we were up to something negative. There was absolutely nothing negative that we were a part of because we had the desire to make something of ourselves. But we didn't know how to prove it to her. That was until she took us to a gynecologist to have us examined, and it wasn't until the doctor told her that we had not been penetrated that she believed us. We were used to being rejected and shot down, so it didn't bother us much. It sure felt good to say, "I told you so," but of course, I said it in my head. No matter what we did, Mom still fussed, cussed, and expressed her dislike for any and everything.

We were finally able to commit to afterschool activities and were allowed to stay after school for the drill team, marching band, and yearbook committee. We were ecstatic! While we were in school, we felt as if we were appreciated. The teachers, staff members, and our peers complimented us and told us what a great job that we did.

Although I felt accepted and validated from people who weren't of the same blood line that I was, it just didn't satisfy me. I was grateful and flattered that people thought so much of me, but I wanted the same from my parents. I had always had very low self-esteem, and it was to the point that I wouldn't look people in the eye, I covered up my smile, and I was so self-conscious of my body type that I was afraid to wear anything that might reveal my shape, or the lack thereof. There were only two instances during high school where I wore a skirt that was above my ankles. I was tired of people saying, "You're so skinny," and my mom saying, "Look at those little stick legs" and "You don't have no shape at all." And the most disheartening thing was that I didn't know if she was trying to hurt me or not. I had expressed on many occasions that I didn't like it when people talked about my weight and looks, but she continued to do it anyway.

# Life Lesson:

It is always a great thing to sit and talk with your children so that you know where they stand on certain issues and if they understand topics like sex. Sex, drugs, and safety issues should be freely discussed so that children/teenagers don't have to go outside of the home and search for answers. When children don't have the answers regarding these topics, they tend to go out and experiment on their own. If as a parent you're not comfortable with discussing these topics, there are many resources in local libraries, counselors, and endless information on the internet that can aid a parent in discussing such topics with their children. If you are unsure if you child is sexually active, then ask them. Even if they don't tell you the truth, don't accuse them!

Build trust with your children by talking about anything and everything, and that will make them more comfortable to share information and feelings with you. Here is a free nugget of information for parents and children alike: it is very possible for a man and woman to date and be in love with each other and not have sex! Although I wasn't taught by my parents about sex, I purpose to teach my child that abstinence is the best and safest option. I never believed in parents providing contraceptives to their children and teaching them that it is "just in case." Although children are taught things, they will still make their own decisions. But we must do our part to ensure that they are equipped with information that allows them to make wiser choices.

# FUTURE PLANS

There were so many things that were going on, and I was looking forward to graduating. I had kept busy with the drill team, marching band and had even met with a couple of recruiters to discuss plans of joining the military to become a military police officer. I wanted to go to college as well and needed some help figuring out which road to take. I met with the guidance counselor at school to see if they could help me to make up my mind.

I think that it was so hard for me to decide because the bottom line was that I wanted to be out of my mom's house and far away. I was so afraid to abandon my twin, cousins, and Grandma, and that fear paralyzed me and caused me not to go forward as quickly with my plans. So in an effort to get some help with my decision, I went to Mom one day to get her opinion, and this is how it went.

"Hey, Ma," I said, "I would like to go to the army to become a police officer or go off to college, out of state, so that I can experience college life and life on my own.

"You and your sister think y'all are so slick," Mom fumed. "I know that y'all have been out looking for an apartment because y'all are so pressed to get out of here. But if you think that y'all are going to succeed, then y'all are wrong and especially because y'all are trying to be sneaky about it. Both of y'all are gonna end up amounting to nothing just like your dumb father. So get out of my face and do what you been doing without my opinion."

And so it was, I did just that.

I continued to succeed in school, took care of the kids, and I did exactly what I had been doing. Only now I did it with more determination than I ever had before. I had gotten better at studying, marching in the band, drilling and leading the cadets as the battalion commander in JROTC, and my work ethic and grades had shown my efforts.

The only thing that I had a hard time gaining control over was the anger. Fear and/or anger had been a normal part of me for as long as I could remember, and every little thing aggravated me. Many people to this day never knew it, but I was moody and irritable and said whatever I wanted to people and expected them to take it however they chose to take it. I was so angry that it oozed out through my voice, and I had become so sarcastic to disguise the anger and played it off as if it was just a joke.

I disliked my life and myself more and more. I didn't love me because I didn't know how to. I would hardly look in the mirror because the person staring back at me, was me, and this image reminded me of everything that Mom said about me. It reminded me of a dumb, skinny, black, stupid young lady who was just like my father. And I wasn't going to amount to anything because he hadn't.

I loved both of my parents, and I didn't think that either of them were any of the names that Mom said. The one very important thing that I thought both of them lacked was loving us enough that we could have believed they did. And that pushed me to do even better! Although I didn't have a desire to have a child when I got older, no matter what happened in my adult life, I was determined not to be the same kind of parent that my parents were.

There was a big drill competition at the armory in Washington, DC, and it was an all-day competition. We looked forward to it every year in JROTC because it was the chance for all of the JROTC cadets from various schools and branches to come together and compete for the trophy and title of champion in armed and unarmed drilling, color guard, and saber team. But most of all, it was our opportunity to meet actual soldiers and to witness one of the greatest shows on earth—the silent-drill team. I had the time of my life at this competition because it was what I wanted to be whenever I had the chance to grow up. I was even happier when

I saw that Mom had come to see us in action. That boosted my confidence way high. I performed and commanded my drill team harder than I ever had before. It also pleased me because my first love was in the building, as he was in the program at a different school, and I got to hang out with him all day. We drilled and placed high in the unarmed-exhibition team that I commanded, although we didn't win first place, and it was so exciting because it was the second-to-the-last drill competition that I would be a part of before I graduated. I had been told on numerous occasions that I was a great leader and I truly enjoyed leading. I had also been told that I had a gift that made people want to be better and do better.

The next big thing that we had to work on was our senior prom, and I had personally looked forward to it because I had never been to a school dance or prom. I mean, I was having a great school year and I had the guy of my dreams that I would be attending it with. And even more special than that was the fact that it would be on his birthday, May 9, 1997.

## *Life Lesson:*

In case you never say the three words "I love you" to your children, be sure that your actions say that you love them. Encourage your children to do better than you ever have and support and congratulate them when they are doing something good. Allow your children to participate in afterschool activities because it helps to develop their gifts and talents and gives them a positive outlet. Children are affected by peer pressure daily and have issues to face that their parents never would've dreamed of. So it is important to understand what children face when they are outside of the house. As the time changes, parenting styles should change as well. The things that worked years ago don't work, and as children grow, then correction and consequences must be adjusted as well.

# PUT OUT

If going to prom were only that easy. We didn't have the money to get our clothes. We had planned to ride in a limo with some of our friends. And how all of this was supposed to happen, I had no idea. All of the money that we had worked for was given to Mom or somehow came up missing from our hiding spots in our room. And we had to solicit some assistance from our father, aunts, and grandmother. Our dad didn't mind helping but had a problem with not being able to see us on the night of the prom to see what his money would be used for.

It didn't make any sense to me that two teens who were doing extremely well in and out of school had to beg to be taken care of by the people who conceived and birthed them. We had to practically beg and plead for the things that we needed. And we had gotten to the point where we didn't even bother asking for the things that we wanted. It had been a confusing time indeed.

As if we weren't busy and stressed enough about wanting to go to our senior prom, we came to discover that the person who owned the condo we were renting wanted us out because the rent hadn't been paid in months. We were devastated because we had been giving money to pay the rent and to help out with whatever else needed to be paid. But obviously that hadn't happened as we thought it had. So here was another pressure that we had to face and another adult problem that we had to figure out how to resolve. Now this one was completely out of our control because we didn't know who the owner was and who the money was supposed to go to.

Of course, everyone was on edge, and Mom was grumpier than ever. And whenever she was grumpy, everyone paid for it. One day, she told us to clean the house, as she always did, but when Twin told her that we had just cleaned the house, she got angry and began to hit her. She backed her into a corner in the kitchen and hit her in the face and head continuously. Twin was trying her best to block her face by putting her arms up over her face and head as she cried, "Stop hitting me...please...just stop hitting me."

I had never been disrespectful to either of my parents regardless of how I felt about what they did. But at that moment, I felt that enough was enough! I was preparing to step into the unknown, and I was afraid because I didn't know what was happening or what had come over me. I stood there while my outward countenance was calm, but inside I was boiling and my temper had just overflowed.

My brows were furrowed, and my hands were clinched tightly by my sides. I trembled at the thought of what I was thinking. All of the anger, resentment, hurt, disappointment and fear had just reached a climax. Slowly, I stepped in front of my mom, looked her in her eyes, and calmly said, "Stop hitting my twin."

She stopped midswing and asked me, "What did you say to me?"

I calmly but sternly said it again. "Stop hitting my twin." I had been afraid of her my entire life and her rages, mood swings, and even physical correction—but no more. I was tired of her beating us whenever she felt like it or just because she wasn't happy with herself or something else.

She lowered her hand, and because she was so calm, I thought she was about to explode on both of us. But she walked away mumbling something incoherent, and I was relieved. I felt horrible because I was unsure if I had crossed the line and had become disrespectful or if I was doing the right thing by standing up and trying to protect my twin.

Mom was attempting to put my twin out of the condo on the same day that this happened, but at least she stopped hitting her. She later came out of nowhere and looked me in the eyes and calmly told me, "You can get out too." At this point, that was the least of my worries because, unfortunately, soon enough all of us would be "getting out too." I wasn't concerned about having to leave the house because I wanted to do that anyway. But I had accomplished what I set out to accomplish. From that day forward, she never hit my twin again. But she did have us put all of our clothes into two big black trash bags and call our aunt to come and pick us up. And we did just that gladly. But Mom ended up simmering down, and she allowed us to come back.

It was now one week away from our eighteenth birthday. Things were still rocky at home, but we couldn't wait to turn eighteen. I felt that I would be an official adult when I turned eighteen. Adults would always say, "You're not grown until you pay some bills up in here." Well I had been doing that for years, so I felt like an adult long before I turned eighteen.

I was still in a relationship with my first love, but things were now a little different between us. I didn't know for what particular reason, but we had grown apart quite a bit. I initially took the blame for that because I knew that my life was a challenge and anyone who loved me for me would have to be as strong as I was or stronger than me. I knew that my life was not smooth sailing, and I expected early on in life that I wouldn't have a serious relationship because he probably wouldn't stand for me being a virgin and probably wouldn't want to deal with what I had to deal with on a daily basis.

He had been hard to get into contact with, and our conversations took more effort than they had before. In the past, we never had to force a conversation or find something to talk about, but our conversations as of late had been awkward and there were plenty of uncomfortable silences. It was so very difficult to deal with because my first love had been one of the main people that I could unload my cares on and maybe it had become more than he could stand. I never wanted to, nor did I ever intend to run anyone off, especially my first love. He was special to me, and I enjoyed every moment that he ever shared with me.

## *Life Lesson:*

Since I've been equipping parents with some information, I'd like to give children some advice. Things don't always go the way that we plan for them to go, and times get hard when we experience different things in our lives. With that being said, it is not okay to be disrespectful to your parents. Although I felt unloved and underappreciated, I made the conscious choice to be respectful. I would never say that this was the easiest thing in the world to accomplish, but I always wanted to be sure that I didn't bring any unwanted hurt, pain, or disappointment to anyone.

Children, you always have to make the decision on how you will react to unwanted and unexpected circumstances. It is never beneficial to dishonor your parents because they are less than what you'd like them to be. I never wanted my parents to be addicted to drugs and watch their character, standards, and morals change. I never wanted my parents to treat me as if I should never have been born or for them to see me on the street and not recognize me, but the fact of the matter is that it happened, and I didn't create the problem, and neither could I have avoided it. Although I harbored so many negative emotions and allowed them to take residence in my heart, I chose to turn the negative thoughts and experiences into positive actions.

And what I find so amazing about this is that choice is no respecter of persons. No matter who you are and what is going on in your life, you have the choice as to how you react or respond to any and every situation in your life. Yes! You read correctly—you control how you react or respond to situations. So choose to find something positive in circumstances and obstacles that you face. There is a life lesson in everything that we experience in our lives. When you overcome obstacles, look back at them and ask yourself what you learned from it so that when you see someone else who is facing the same challenge or obstacle, then you will be able to share some wisdom with them. It is then that winning and overcoming becomes a more familiar cycle, rather than violence and crime.

# DON'T PUT OUT

With all of the excitement that had been going on in my busy little world, I was now turning eighteen, and that was enough to keep me excited for a while. I was so happy that I lived to see eighteen and was excited that my age meant that it was close to move-out time, or so I hoped.

Prom plans were still in the works, and Grandma ended up being the one who picked up the slack. She made sure that we had everything that we needed and the limo and everything else had been finalized, and we were so excited. My dad and aunts also played a very major part in the preparation plans, and they contributed to make sure that we had money to go out and eat dinner and to enjoy ourselves.

The day had come, April 19, 1997, and we were eighteen years of age. We didn't get to do anything fun or go anywhere, but we were of legal age now. We didn't have any other reason for wanting to be of legal age, except that we could move out of the house. . We stayed in the house because we didn't have any money to go anywhere or do anything. It was truly a big deal for us anyhow.

One thing that disappointed me more than anything was that my first love hadn't called me all day long. Things had been different between us, but never once did I think that he wouldn't even call me on my special day. He had been there for me for the past two years, and he knew everything that I had been through. He was an intimate part of my life, and I just didn't understand what was going on with us. But then I thought that it was because I wasn't having sex, so maybe I wasn't the girl for him after all. Despite my thoughts and the tension that had developed between us, we remained a couple.

It had been told to me many times that "guys have needs," and if that was the case, then all it took was one word from him and our relationship would have ended promptly. I was determined not to lose my virginity because it wouldn't make anything in my life less complicated and I wasn't ready to just give myself away, even though I loved him. Love wasn't enough for me to share the one thing that I did have control over. So in my mind, there was no negotiation there.

One of our mutual friends called me to wish me a happy birthday and informed me that she had seen my love with someone at the movie theater. There was no reason for my friend to lie to me, and since he hadn't called me or anything, it wasn't very hard to believe. I was hurting beyond belief. I had already put a lot of my time, trust, and heart into the relationship, and I felt like he was all that I had. But I see that he obviously didn't feel the same way.

I was hurt and angry, and when he finally contacted me two full days later, it was on and poppin'. After I confronted him about it, I cried, and naturally, he denied. He stated that he wasn't feeling well and that's why he hadn't called me. I told him that I didn't care if he was somewhere writing another book of the Bible and that it was simply unacceptable. He apologized, but he wasn't let off of the hook that easily. One thing that I didn't tolerate from anyone was lying, and I had been a strong-willed young lady because life taught me to be that way. I didn't believe that lying to anyone, for any reason, was a good thing. I had been an honest person, even though it got me in trouble sometimes.

From that point on, things were even more rocky, but we still loved each other. I was in no way lowering my standards, and I was in no way going to tolerate any mess just because I wasn't having sex with him. He still didn't have the right to treat me badly or any kind of way. I knew that I still deserved respect, and I was going to get it no matter what the cost. I had fought all of my life for acceptance and respect, and I wouldn't sell myself short. Our relationship was now strained because I told him exactly how I felt. One thing that my mom still says to me this very day, is that I wasn't a liar and I've always spoken my mind on any matter and wasn't afraid of the consequences.

Things at home were not as frustrating because I was so focused on prom, my last drill meet, and then graduation in June. As the weeks passed by and I was staying after school for drill team practice, I had grown closer with one of the young men on my drill team. We spent some time talking at the school and on the phone, and I had grown to like him very much. One day, during rehearsals, I went inside of the building to use the restroom and saw him in the hall. We stood and talked for a little while. In the midst of us talking, he leaned in and kissed me. I was surprised but not disappointed. It just so happened that another young man entered the hallway and said, "Ooooh, I'm gonna tell." I felt horrible, but it wasn't something that was planned. I didn't have a clue as to how I would respond to this kiss, and life had gotten just a little more complicated.

# *Life Lesson:*

Children today face so many different types of pressure. They are faced with pressures, like whether or not to have premarital sex at an early age, smoking cigarettes and experimenting with drugs and alcohol, their sexuality, and maintaining a reputation. Whether you have children or not, be a positive role model for a child by being there to listen to them. Times have changed, and oftentimes parents don't understand the challenges that children face because they don't take the time to talk to their children and listen to them.

One thing that I've learned about children is that if you start at an early age and allow them to trust you, they will talk, and they will talk about anything. Younger children and teenagers alike don't always know how to express themselves and explain the pressure that they are facing. Don't downplay their feelings and cast them off so easily. Oftentimes, teenagers aren't as open with their parents because it hasn't been a normal practice or the teenagers feel like their parents either can't relate to them or they don't understand them. Take some time and give your children your undivided attention. Allow them to talk and to do it freely! Be patient with your children and offer solutions because if they are struggling with problems they've never faced before, then more than likely, they don't have a solution for them.

# PROM NIGHT NIGHTMARE

As time went on, I continued to talk with this young man and had grown closer to him. I found out that he was interested in me, and I was in him, but I was still in a relationship with my first love, so this new excitement wasn't going any further than a friendship. There is no way that I was willing to even attempt to juggle two different relationships at the same time. It was disrespectful and I wasn't interested in even appearing like I was some sort of player. So, I did end up telling my love that another young man had kissed me. Not much came out of it because it wasn't initiated by me and it didn't happen again as long as I was with him. Our relationship was already strained at this point and from my birthday until prom, it seemed as though we were forcing our relationship to work. But, something just wouldn't allow us to let it go. I especially didn't want to let it go because I enjoyed the closeness, the conversations by phone and face-to- face and the fact that somebody loved me and told me that he loved me every day.

Prom time had finally arrived. The day before prom, Uncle took us to get our hair done and took us around to make sure that we saw our dad. Dad wasn't happy that he wouldn't be there to take pictures or see us in our prom dresses. I thought that it'd be more fitting if he was upset that he would miss his daughters' big night than being sour that he had given us some money but wouldn't see what his money had been spent on. And although my mom worked, she had bills to pay to keep a roof over our heads so she didn't have the extra money to spare on our prom. So, my aunt Lissa was kind enough to understand the importance of one of the biggest days of our lives and she purchased our prom dress for us. I don't know if it was a good thing, but at this point in my life, I was so used to feeling like I wasn't priority in my parents' lives. It was never about us and we were always the topic of our parents' frustration. This may not have been how my parent's felt, but it sure is how I felt.

But Mom was there the night of prom and helped us to get dressed, and she took pictures of us before we left. I was so happy that she was interested in helping us to get dressed and seeing us off for the evening. Unfortunately, Twin's date never showed up, and we left without him. When I saw the disappointment on her face, I quickly became angry and extremely disappointed. It was disheartening to see that someone close to us, other than a family member could disappoint us to this degree. When my date arrived, he was oh-so-finely dressed in a nice tuxedo and had a beautiful corsage for me to wear on my arm. I was dressed in a long off-white dress, with beads on it, and the top portion that was above the breast was see-through. The dress was fitting and was almost ankle length, with a slit on one of the front legs. I felt confident, and I looked good as well.

There were six or eight of us in the limo, and we went to dinner first and then arrived at the prom. As we entered the ballroom, the JROTC saber team had their swords drawn. Guy No. 2, whom I liked so much and who kissed me, just happened to be standing at the entrance. As we walked by him, I felt horrible, and then someone lowered his sword and slapped me on the butt with it. I didn't bother turning around because I already felt awkward with two gentlemen that I felt deeply for being in the same space.

Before this time, I never knew that you could actually be in love with more than one person at the same time. The topic of being in love with more than one person at the same time is debatable, and I think that it will always be. Both of them were totally different, and I enjoyed and cared for them for who they were. My first love was of my height, light skinned, and brown eyed, while the second young man was taller than me, dark-skinned, and had dark eyes. Both of them were strikingly handsome, and I had grown to love Guy No. 2. It was hard being a teenager!

It just so happened that every time that I was standing around in the hall talking to Guy No. 2, his funny and crazy friend named Leroy would just happen to pop up everywhere! I thought it mighty strange that he seemed to be everywhere that I was. Leroy and I were very good friends, and we joked and laughed a lot. But that was the extent of our relationship. He was a total blast to have around. I often hung out with Leroy, and I knew his family and he knew mine. I thought that he was handsome, and I enjoyed being around him. I had almost put him on stalker status but thought better of it because he was showing up everywhere that I was, but I'll delve into that later.

Back to my prom, it was a total blast! We walked in and commenced to gettin' down with the git down! We danced fast and slow, the ambiance was so perfect, and it had been one of the best experiences of my life. I and my first love had been to a military ball together and had dined and danced together and had almost as much fun as we had on prom night. My first love made it a night to remember, literally. When the night ended, the limo took everyone to their perspective homes.

Everything ended well—that is until my love arrived home. He had called to let me know that he was home. And just as we always did, we spent a couple of hours talking on the phone, which was when the opposite of heaven broke loose. My love and his little brother had gotten into some sort of an argument, so the little brother decided to make me aware of some things that I hadn't been privy to.

I came to find out that my love had lied to me about his age. Okay, so he was a year or two younger than he told me he was. I never saw it coming, and I felt betrayed by the person that I least expected. No, the age thing wasn't a big deal, but the lying was. And the fact that my love never came out and told me whether it was true or not was even more baffling. All that he could say was, "I will tell her what I want when I want." He didn't even say it to me, but he spoke to his brother the entire time. That surely wasn't the straw that broke the camel's back.

More important than what had been previously discussed, his brother was in the background, saying, "And won't you tell her how all of these gay dudes are always hanging out over here?" All that he could say was, "Really?" or "Won't you just shut up" or "Whatever." I had to have him run that by me again!

Everything that I was familiar and comfortable with slowly slipped away from me, and I really wasn't sure how to handle the news. And the fact that he didn't deny it worried me even further. After a while of prodding, he finally said, "That is a lie." At that point, I didn't know what to believe or if anything that he said was true. All of the times that he said "I love you," "I miss you," and "I want to be with you" were probably lies as well. It had been too much for me to handle, so I ended the phone conversation so that my head could stop spinning.

From that point on, he expected me to be the same. Whenever we did talk, which was few and far in between, my answers were short. Then he had the nerve to ask me "Where does all of this negativity coming from?" And I thought that he couldn't possibly be serious. He was still making plans for us to be together and get married and blah blah blah, and there were more rumors going around about his sexuality and his affiliation with the homosexual community. I couldn't prove it, and I didn't believe it; nevertheless, our relationship slowly dwindled.

## *Life Lesson:*

Things aren't always what they seem and the only thing that you can do when being in a relationship with another human being is to trust them. I spent so much time trying to dig in and understand people and how their minds work and never once did I sit back and just trust in anyone 100%. I'd always been so afraid to live life because I was unconsciously awaiting the next disappointment. But I've learned that being so cautious and sitting back waiting on disappointments to happen, that it caused me to build up a wall that no one could break down. It caused me to live in fear and not open up too much to anyone for fear that I would be disappointed again. Disappointments come in many different forms and not that every day is filled with them, but they will happen and we must learn to press on and trust in people. Don't build relationships with the expectation that they will disappoint you, do build them knowing that human beings are not perfect. I found myself disappointed quite a bit because I expected more of a person than they could give me. It is okay to let your guard down and experience life through genuine relationships and don't let disappointment wrap its ugly arms around you and keep you from living a fear-free life.

# SCARED TO FINISH

It was now time for the JROTC drill meet at Parkdale High School. The drill meet at the armory was great, but this was the Super Bowl of drill meets. I was the commander, and being a senior now, it was my last hoorah, so to speak. We had gone to the drill meet with great expectation because the rivalry between Fairmont Heights and Parkdale was like the Washington Redskins and the Dallas Cowboys rivalry. It had been a battle between the two schools before I attended Fairmont, and I'm sure it still was long after I graduated.

We not only wanted to have a good time, but we wanted to kick butt and win first place in the process. And we did just that! It had been the sweetest victory ever, and I remember it like it was yesterday. Our drill team executed each move with precision and accuracy, and we brought home the first-place trophy. That moment had been the greatest accomplishment of my life, and neither mommy nor daddy was there to share in it. I just wish they could see all of the great things that we were capable of and that we did in school and out.

But at the long-awaited age of eighteen, it was still like I was six years old. The raw emotions and desires for guidance were the same as they had been years ago. And although I felt like a child, I felt like an adult as well due to all of the responsibilities that I had. Nevertheless, time stood still for no one, and I was so confused about life, but I had to keep it moving. So the next big thing that I was looking forward to was my graduation day. Graduation was the single most important accomplishment of my life thus far, and I was so excited to have come to this point in my life.

Another big day had come, and we were getting dressed for our high-school graduation. It was June 1997, and we were so very excited! We got up early and dressed, and this time everyone was going to be there to see us walk across the stage. Mom, Grandma, uncles, and cousins were all in attendance, and it felt great to know that they were there for us.

When my name was called, I walked across that stage so proudly but was horrified at the same time. I know this may sound crazy to some—but school was my place of peace and happiness, and it was ending. It was the place that I loved to go so that I could get away from the ruckus and the disarray at home. There were no major responsibilities like bathing people and cooking and sweeping, vacuuming, and so forth. I could just spend time studying and being me.

I was horrified at the thought of how I would have to spend my days now. I was afraid that things would get worse and that the work was now going to double. I didn't feel like I had my own identity or personality at home because we were always being screamed and yelled at and being cussed at and ordered around like robots. We all know that robots didn't have any say-so in anything; they simply did what they were told and couldn't speak a word otherwise. But at school, people asked my opinion on matters, and my friends and even teachers allowed me to lead and make choices, and that was the type of person that I was. I had been a leader for many years, and I believed that I was good at it. After we all had received our diplomas, we met up backstage and cried our eyes out. I cried because I was happy, but mostly because I didn't know what my next step in life was. I had a desire to go into the military and to college. But I didn't have the chance to do either because of the responsibility that I had. And most importantly, I couldn't stand to leave my twin. She had always had it a little rougher than I did, as far as Mom beating her and slapping her in the face because she looked like our father. So I didn't know if leaving her behind was the right choice. Therefore, I continued to do what I had been doing for years, and that was to take care of everyone else's needs and someday hope to accomplish my goals.

I had so many great plans for myself, but deep down inside, I didn't believe that I could accomplish any of them. I wanted to believe in myself, and I constantly spoke the words, but Mom's voice spoke louder. All that I could think about was her saying, "Y'all gonna be just like your no good, stupid, lazy, trifling father since y'all wanna sneak off and see him when he ain't doing nothing for y'all." Since I had heard that so many times, that's what I believed. Even to this very day I still don't understand how I was an honor-roll student my entire school life, and at the same time I still thought that I was stupid.

Most of my friends were going off to college, and some decided to stay back and work after high school. As for me, I didn't have the choice. I did go out and speak with recruiters to get more information for the armed forces. I still struggled with whether or not I was going to follow through with it and fulfill my dreams or if I would just stick around at home. My grandma had been really sick on and off, and I hated to leave her there as well.

# *Life Lesson:*

We only have this one life to live on earth, and things are going to happen in your life and you're not going to be sure what to do about it. Things will come your way and you won't know how to handle them, but the good thing about being free and still having breath in your body is that when we don't make the best decisions, we can change them. Sometimes people have regrets because they spend their lives doing things that don't please them and they spend time surrounded by people who don't make them better. Don't be afraid to step out and fulfill your dreams because you don't want to look back 10 years later and wish that you had done things that you never got the chance to do. Not all decisions are easy, but the only way that we learn is when we do. So step out on faith and do the things that your heart desires to do. Be responsible in all that you do and since you only live once on earth, have fun and fulfill your dreams!

# THROWN OUT

In the middle of the year 1998, we received numerous phone calls from the gentleman who owned the condo. Apparently, the rent hadn't been paid in months, and we were in hot water. Neither Grandma, Twin, nor myself could figure out why the rent hadn't been paid because all of us had contributed money since we had moved into the condo. And what I personally couldn't understand was where the money went, considering all of the money that had come up missing out of mine and Twin's room and all of the times that we give almost our entire paychecks to Mom.

We were constantly scrounging up a few dollars to buy groceries, to pay the phone bill, and to get the personal items that we needed. Everyone in the house was working, except the younger kids and Grandma, so there was no reason for the bills not to be paid. But the reality was that they weren't paid, and this was a problem that I could not fix myself.

Twin and I were now working in retail at Filene's Basement in downtown DC and were bringing home most of our paychecks. We had to deduct money for transportation, which was the wonderful Metro train and bus, and for personal items that we needed. We were now responsible working adults, and a family friend who also lived in our building got us the jobs at Filene's Basement. We were so grateful that he had looked out for us and helped us. He even helped Mom get a job there as well. So the three of us were working at the same place, yet the bills still weren't paid.

The moment I and Twin heard the bad news about us having to move out of the condo in a very short amount of time, like one week, we went downstairs to tell our family friend what had happened. We went to him because we looked up to him as a responsible adult, and we needed some help. We were so scared because we didn't know where all of us would go. We were definitely ashamed of having to move so quickly because anytime this sort of situation happened, it wasn't hard to figure out that someone was slacking in paying the bills.

Mr. K was so kind, and he did his best to console us. But when Mom found out that we talked to him about it, she was furious with us. It had not been our intention to embarrass her or anyone else for that matter; we were just afraid, and we needed someone to talk to. But again, Mom wasn't concerned about our feelings.

It was so sad to see her standing in the kitchen and clutching the phone in both hands while crying and begging the owner to give her some more time. It tore my heart apart, but at the same time I was so angry. We could see her defeat when she hung up the phone, and she turned to us and sadly said, "He wants us out of here."

I wanted so badly to ask, "Why weren't you paying the rent?" and "If you needed more money, why didn't you say so?" I would've asked for more hours at work if that was what was needed. I felt horrible because I knew that my mom had a problem, and although I was angry, I knew that she needed some help. But it was too late, and we didn't know where we would go.

Mom told us that we needed to learn to shut our mouths and keep other people out of our household business. All that we ever tried to do was help. There were constantly people who had been aware of our household business. Mom had to deal with social workers popping up at the house any time that they wanted to because we had three of my little cousins there and she had been in the process of adopting them for years. So there had always been someone in our business. And for those who hadn't been in it before, they would surely be in it soon.

We had no money for a moving truck, and if we did have the money, where would we move the stuff to? My mom ordered us to call our aunts on our father's side to see if they could contact our father so that Twin and I would have a place to go. That thought was really heartwarming, and any type of good thoughts or affection that my mom showed toward me was welcomed. We packed all of the clothes and shoes that we could into two huge trash bags and left with our aunt when she came to pick us up.

It had been hard to concentrate, sleep, eat, or work because I was so worried about what would happen to my cousins, grandmother, and even my mom. I love and have always loved my family, despite what has happened in my life. My grandma was bedridden and needed a lot of care and attention. She had been in and out of the hospital for high blood pressure, diabetes, heart trouble and strokes. She had had a triple bypass surgery and another bypass surgery before that, and the stress was not good for her. Before we left, we hugged her and told her that we loved her and we didn't know when we would see her again. My heart ached, and I was so confused and at a loss. I didn't know what would happen to my cousins, and I wanted the best care for them. I had begun to lose sleep again, and worry was causing me to become physically sick. I had seen my mom act many different ways, and I had seen her in many different moods, but I had never seen her so defeated. She seemed helpless and looked like she was going to just give up. But now it was her time to fix the problem and take care of everyone. I felt so bad for her because I didn't think that she knew how. She had been absent for so long that it seemed overwhelming for her to have to step back up to the adult plate and bring it home for the team. But I had done all that I could do at that point. We hugged Mom and left.

It was a sad time when we returned to the neighborhood a couple of days later and saw some of our stuff straddled across the sidewalk in front of the building. And it was too embarrassing to get out of the car to salvage what we wanted from the street. I had seen people lose their homes before, but never once did I think that it would happen to us. Mom, Grandma, and the little ones moved to Northwest DC with one of my uncles, while I and twin continued to work and moved to Forestville, Maryland, with our aunt.

The guy that I had been dating on the job had his own place and invited me over. We had gone out a couple of times, and I liked him a lot. He was funny, had a job, but he also had a child. That was not something that I wanted in a relationship, but I had grown to like him a lot, and he was the only one who had been giving me some attention. Before we were evicted, I told Mom I was going over his house to spend the night, and she wasn't very happy about that. She turned to me and said, "Are you going to lose your virginity now?"

I told her that I didn't know what I was going to do and that he seemed like he cared for me. So I went and spent the night and lost my virginity. It was not pleasant, but I cared even more deeply for him now that we had come together. I made a decision based on pure emotion, and I knew that I wasn't ready to give myself away, but I had truly been emotionally unstable.

He brought me over to his house plenty of times, and we would ride the train together to work, but we didn't go very many places in public together. And when he did bring me to his house, he'd leave me in his bedroom with the television to keep me company while he would entertain his friends in the front room. That didn't help my self-esteem any, but he had been the only one who had given me the affection that I wanted, which was any affection at all. I thought that losing my virginity would satisfy my need for affection, but it didn't! And just because I thought that he cared for me, I thought that it was the right thing to do. After the situation with my first love, I thought that it was something that I had to do in order to keep this one.

He'd be missing in action for a couple of days at a time, and then he'd show up to whisk me off to his house, and because I really did love him, I accepted what little he gave. No one ever told me what the "right thing" was to do, so I tried stuff for myself and had to figure out if it felt right. I knew that this wasn't right because he didn't treat me the same way that I treated him. I was faithful to him because I was in a relationship with him. I was available whenever he called and hoped that he would be as available to me one day.

Needless to say we dated, or the lack thereof, until some time in 1998, when he left me a voicemail on my phone that said, "Look, I don't think that this is working out between us." It was a bright and sunny day when I got the message, and he was supposed to be at an amusement park with whomever he had gone with. He made it his business to call me in the midst of his fun day.

Here was yet another major letdown, and his excuse that I was "not being there enough" for him was a total cop-out. But I, in the end, was the foolish one because I gave all of myself to him and didn't demand respect or anything else from him. One thing that the comedian Eddie Murphy said in one of his shows was, "You get what you give." I just thought that he was the one to fulfill my desire for male affection. Little did I know that I was connected to him in a whole new way.

# GREATEST LOSS

The year 1997 and the first half of 1998 had been rough for us. After being evicted from our home and seeing my grandma's health slowly deteriorate, it was hard to get a good grip on life. I honestly didn't know whether I was coming or going. The only person in my life whom I felt was consistent and who truly loved me had quickly begun to grow ill.

Grandma was a strong and smart woman, and she kept our family together. She was always the one to plan events so that the family could get together and so that there was some type of fun and happiness among everyone. She taught me how to cook at the age of six, how to iron, how to clean, and how to balance a checkbook.

Out of all of the things that my grandma taught me, the most memorable lesson that I learned from her was how to play spades. She sat my twin and I down and taught us the art of the game and taught us to always take it seriously. We were taught how to play spades at the age of six, and to this day we are serious about playing spades. Although we thought that it was "just a card game," there was no such thing to her. When you sat down and played, it was always all or nothing.

Grandma spent a lot of time loving us and teaching us some very important life skills. Whenever she was healthy, she nurtured us and made sure that we had the bare essentials of life.

In June of 1998, my grandma passed away. She had been in the hospital for about two weeks, and Twin and I were called while at work and were told that our grandmother had taken a turn for the worse and that the family was to report to the hospital immediately.

Upon our arrival, Grandma was in bad shape. Her organs were slowly failing, and she seemed so helpless. My heart hurt so badly, and I didn't want to even imagine what I would do without her. And it wasn't just about me, but I wondered what the entire family would do without her. During visiting hours that day, she could only have two visitors in her room at once, and I unintentionally changed that rule. Only one family member at a time came in to visit because I held her hand for hours and refused to leave her side. After hours of sitting in the hospital and watching my grandma immobile and unresponsive, we returned to our respective homes. Twin and I were staying with our aunt in Forestville, Maryland, and were very grateful that she had reached out and took us in.

The next day, we went to the hospital to see her, and we thought that it was a pure miracle. Grandma was sitting up, and she was more alert than I had ever seen her. I brushed her long silky salt- and-pepper hair and kissed her cheek and asked her if she was going home with us. She was laughing and talking to us, and things seemed as normal as normal was. She looked at me bright eyed and bubbly and shook her head no. I didn't understand why she didn't want to come home. I mean the hospital staff had been nice, but I didn't want to make a hospital my home, and I didn't understand why she would want to either. I told her that I'd be sure to take good care of her.

We laughed and talked with the family, and all was going extremely well. I assumed that in a day or two, the doctors would allow her to go home. So we spent the entire day with her and kissed her good night. I went home with so much peace and joy, and all that I could do was smile. But another thing I didn't understand was how she was so alert and happy and healthy looking, yet the very next day she passed away.

I didn't know what to do with myself and I had an extremely hard time coping. This point in my life was definitely bittersweet because my grandmother was going to be greatly missed and her death caused me to view life in a different way. My twin and I had finally reached a point where we had gotten our first apartment together and didn't have to be in an environment where we would be cursed out, yelled at and called negative names. It was definitely a time of refreshing and peace but definitely wasn't celebrated because of my grandmother and her illness and death. I was so worried about my mother and how she was going to cope with her mother's death. But, I didn't know how to help her either. I loved my mom and wanted nothing but the best for her. Although I was grown and out of the house, I still didn't know what to do with myself. I felt so alone because my grandma was everything to me. Children have special bonds with their siblings and parents, but there is a different bond between a grandparent and their grandchild. She was always the one who made everything all right, even though everything wasn't all right. My grandma found something positive in every situation. She may have fussed and cussed about some things, but she always made any and everything all right. There was always a positive in the negative.

I didn't understand death, and I wasn't sure who was going to love me now. Whenever I felt really down and out, I could always go and hug or talk to my grandma and she'd tell me everything would be all right and would help me to see the positive side in any situation. And now she was gone. I could never describe the feeling that I had when I realized that I wasn't going to be able to hear her voice and see her stomach shake whenever she laughed. I felt sad for my mom as well because she did take the initiative to take my grandma in and make sure that she had a place to live.

I didn't know how any of us would make it, but somehow, life went on. Many of my nights were sleepless, and my days consumed with staring into nowhere and trying to understand what had just happened and why. I cried and cried until I couldn't cry anymore, and it just felt like time stopped. I didn't understand life, and I didn't understand death.

# SHOCK OF 1999

After I had been dumped by the man that I gave my virginity to, I had truly been down and out. And the one thing that I neglected to do was to take some time to get to know and love myself. I didn't know who I was or what I wanted. I just knew that I wanted to be hugged, comforted, complimented, and just loved. So I continued to search in what I later found were the wrong places and in the wrong way for the love and affection that I longed for. I had never been told that I meant the world to my mom or dad, and if you don't get the love at home, you tend to go outside of home to find it. It was definitely not the right thing to do, but when you don't know better, you tend not to do better. So on to the next guy I went. He was yet another guy that I felt deeply for that didn't feel as deeply for me. I was a mature young lady who knew how to take care of children, the elderly, and how to run a household, but it was hard to find someone who was on my maturity level. I had gotten into what I thought was a relationship because he had shown some interest in me.

One thing that I didn't understand was how I had such low self-esteem and didn't love myself, yet there had always been some guy who was interested in me. I later figured that guys can definitely tell when a young lady has low self-esteem, and I attracted only the guys that I deserved to attract. I never did anything to try and attract men to me, but I always seemed to attract them to me somehow.

While searching for love and affection, I continued to have sex and got pregnant. I didn't try to get pregnant, and a child of my own had not been in my future plans. I never wanted children, and what I didn't realize was that I shouldn't have had sex before marriage. The both of us were young and weren't ready for a child, and so that added extra stress and confusion to my life. The father of my child had not been very supportive, but his family was absolutely wonderful. They were supportive and were always willing to help me emotionally.

His mom would always tell me that she cared for me and that she was praying for me, and she would occasionally invite me to go to church with her. I told her that one day I would. But I didn't feel as if I was good enough to step into anyone's church. Although I had not grown up in a church, and I didn't know anything about God, Jesus, or church, I knew that the way that I was living wasn't right. I didn't feel right about my actions, and I didn't have any peace. At the time, I didn't even know much about having peace, and what I did know was that I didn't feel happy about having sex outside of marriage, or drinking alcohol. I had missed my parents and my grandmother so much, and I didn't know how to deal with anything. Although I was angry, and hurt, I still felt so empty.

The mother of the guy who got me pregnant told me that she had overheard her son say that he had purposely put a hole in the condom so I'd get pregnant. I never verified whether that story was true or not. I was ashamed, angry, and embarrassed because I wasn't into church, but I knew that I wasn't supposed to be having sex before marriage anyway, and to know that it was done purposely angered me to no end. There was just a gnawing in my heart, and I felt so guilty each time I'd lay down, and the guilt made me shrink away and want to hide from anyone who knew God. I was stressed out every day, and I was barely supporting myself.

I was seven weeks pregnant, and one day, while I was at work, I started to cramp and bleed badly. I was rushed to the hospital and learned that I had miscarried. It had been a painful experience both physically and emotionally. The pain and emptiness that I felt was unlike any other pain that I had ever felt before. Although I wasn't ready for a baby and wasn't overjoyed with the way that the child had been conceived, I felt a sense of love for my child. The moment I went to the doctor and saw the little heart beating on the screen, I had become attached.

I was continuously stressing over the pregnancy, and I knew that the father wasn't ready either. But just as I had done in any other situation in my life, I had to grow up even more and take responsibility for my actions. As a mature young adult, I accepted the consequences of my actions quickly, and although I was stressing, I had been steadily preparing for the child that was growing inside of me. I had a great career in banking, and I had my own apartment, so I knew that I had to make some new adjustments in order to accommodate the baby.

Every other day, I had been worried about how my life had already been changed, and although I had a life growing inside of me, I still felt so alone and unloved. I had never planned to have any children of my own because I wanted to live for myself and find out who I was. I felt as though I had raised all of the children that I needed to, and I didn't have a desire to spend the rest of my life raising a child.

I was only nineteen and was so resentful, angry, and sad, and I didn't know how to let the negative aggression out. When I heard that voice say that there was more, was this the "more" that it meant? I was still unhappy and in search of myself and love, so I hated to see what more was ahead of me. I cared for the father of my child deeply, but he wasn't there for me during the pregnancy or during the loss of our child, and I had experienced a new level of hurt. I was still seeking affection during this hard time in my life. My body was in pain, and my mind and heart was also.

I had to figure out how to heal on my own, and it was extremely hard. To know that I had a life that had been growing inside of me and then not understand why I lost it was a hard pill to swallow, and the only option that I had was the same as it had been all of my life, and that was to hopefully figure it out one day and for now it was simply to keep moving forward. And though it was a long and confusing road, I'd been able to move on.

# A NEW CHAPTER

After my relationship, or what I thought was a relationship, had ended, I decided to just give up on trying to find love through men. I then decided to sit back and relax and make time for myself. I had decided that it would no longer be an option of me giving myself to anyone, physically or emotionally.

I gave in and finally visited church. I began attending the Believer's Worship Center/Reach Out for Life Christian Center in Forestville, Maryland, where Bishop Larry and Pastor Delphine Jordan delivered power-packed teachings weekly. I thoroughly enjoyed myself! Since I hadn't grown up in a church, and none of my family members did, it was different, but I was open to new experiences and possibilities.

I had hit rock bottom and was tired of seeking approval in men, alcohol, and clubs. I was tired of having sex and still feeling empty, guilty, and unsatisfied inside. I was also tired of picking up a glass of alcohol while dancing the night away at a club and trying to gain the attention of men with tight jeans, high heels, and shirts on that exposed my flat stomach and belly chain. I was tired of getting made up and dolled up for the wrong reasons.

So one crisp fall night, I was sitting in the church when I kept getting a nervous feeling in my stomach. I thought that I was about to be punished or struck by lightning for just having spent the evening at the club and in bed with the same man that I told myself I wouldn't spend the night with or for the drink that I escorted around the club just the week before. I thought it also could've been from the dancing that I did just the night before I went to church.

I replayed in my mind how I had spent the majority of the night shaking, bouncing, and grinding on any man who wanted to dance with me. The men would look my size two frame up and down, lick their lips, and ask me to dance. And because someone finally seemed interested in my chocolate-colored skin, long legs, flat stomach, pushed-up breasts, and waist-length thick brown hair, it seemed like satisfaction was on the way for me. But I later realized that each and every one of those men was under the influence of more than their needed share of watered- down alcoholic beverages. I came to the conclusion, based on experience, that everyone in the club looks good to you when you are drunk.

When the message had concluded at church, and the bishop called out for those who didn't know Jesus, I quickly gathered my belongings and exited the church against the ushers' wishes for everyone to be seated until the conclusion of service or benediction. I was so afraid and decided that I wouldn't go back to that church because I didn't want to be punished for all of the wrong that I'd done.

A few weeks passed by, and I stayed as clear as I could from the church, although I could look out of my bedroom window and see the entire church building, which was a quick forty-five seconds from my door to its front door. I was determined to work through all of my feelings and issues on my own, and the more that I promised myself that I wouldn't do something, the more I did it. I was truly fed up with me continuously disappointing myself and trying to figure everything out on my own.

My twin and I shared a two-bedroom basement apartment in the apartment complex right across the street from the church, but she had moved out and had moved in with her boyfriend, who is now her husband, and I had moved into a one bedroom apartment in the front of the same complex. At that point I really had plenty of time to sit in peace and quiet and hear clearly and think about everything. But there was so much to think about that I had become increasingly agitated and overwhelmed with life again.

So the following week, I found myself sitting in the midst of the congregation at the church that I told myself I would not be going back to. And at the end of the service, the pastor stood up again and invited people to come up to the front if they desired to know Jesus. I had gotten that nervous feeling before, only this time it was ten times worse.

I was severely agitated because I wondered why a man would stand up at the front of the church week after week and pry into people's lives, like mine, and then invite them to know Jesus. The entire time any one of the speakers preached their sermons, I felt as if they were standing in the foyer of the church and peeking through my window. They spoke directly to me, no matter what the message was that they were delivering. I felt tired, agitated, and nervous, and the feeling wouldn't go away. And then the pastor had the nerve to stand there and say, "Whoever it is that God is waiting for, come on up here because we're going to wait for you."

I didn't want to be rude and walk out like I did the last time, so I sat and I looked around just as everyone else was doing. There were ministers standing at the front of the church, waiting to pray for those who had the nerve to come forward. I sat uncomfortably in my seat, and I shook, literally. I was so nervous, and I couldn't contain myself. So after some more coaxing from my stomach and my extremities, I gathered my belongings and looked at the exit as I walked to the front of the church.

Once I made it to the front of the church, I stood there, snot crying, with my hands lifted up because I was tired and was at the lowest point in my life. I held my hands up in total surrender, and I gave my life to Jesus that very night. I had tried to do it all on my own but was unsuccessful, so I was ready to give it all to someone else to handle, and his track record was way better than mine when it came to taking on people's burdens and actually making them better. I could no longer carry that weight on my own. I was only one hundred pounds soaking wet, but I walked through life feeling as if I were two hundred pounds.

I confessed with my mouth and believed in my heart that Jesus was the Son of God and that he died and was raised from the dead and that he did it all just for me. I didn't know much about heaven or hell, but I just knew that hell had frozen over because Jesus had accepted me and he had done it just as I was. He didn't cast me away because of my behaviors, and I didn't have anything to lose. I no longer had to try and clean myself up, and he still died for me.

Later that night, I felt as if I had been ripped off. I didn't feel any different when I had accepted Jesus, and I thought that there was supposed to be some spooky jookie feeling, but I hadn't felt a thing. Late one night, as I lay frustrated in bed, that same sweet and quiet little voice said, "There's more." I was so tired of hearing that line, but for the first time since I first heard it, I believed it! I felt like I couldn't go any lower than I was, so there was no other way but up for me.

The more I visited the church and actively listened to the Word being preached, the more I applied what they told me to apply to my life, and it was then that I started to feel different. I started to feel more confident in myself and my ability to become someone great. I had always been promoted on any job that I had been on and in school, but I still felt unworthy growing up and thought that I would amount to nothing just like my mom said. But those thoughts were slowly fading away. The thoughts still came into my mind, but I responded differently to them. I did still struggle at times, but I kept hearing and hearing, and to this very day I'm still hearing the Word of God.

I hadn't grown up in church so I didn't know how I was supposed to feel after giving my life to the Lord, and I had seen on television and had heard stories of people yelling and screaming and falling out when they gave their lives to the Lord, so naturally I thought that this would never work out. I knew that I had quite the road ahead of me, but I was motivated again, and I was ready for the challenge.

# THE LIGHT AT THE END OF MY TUNNEL

Through all of my frustration and hurt, I had begun to talk to one of my good friends. If you all remember, I had that crazy friend named Leroy who was always around and was always clowning. We had been out of touch for about a year, and he had joined the Marine Corps. We had begun to talk on the phone just so we could get to know each other even better. We spent hours and hours just laughing, joking, and talking about our challenges and goals. I had a sneaking suspension that Leroy had an interest in me, but that thought was quickly dismissed because up until this point, he hadn't said anything to me about a relationship, which was so refreshing. He had just shown me that he enjoyed talking to me and getting to know me better. I must admit that there was a small attraction because we had worked closely together in JROTC and he had come over to the house to play cards and to hang out with me and some other friends.

Leroy was hilarious, smart, and handsome. He was easy to talk to, and we talked about any and everything. I had given up on searching for a man to complete me, and I was determined to be complete on my own. The road wasn't easy, but I had to do something. We both voiced our frustrations with dating and were focused on doing better in our lives. Another thing that we had in common was that we wrote poetry. We spent some time reading our original creations to each other over the phone.

Leroy was living in South Carolina on the Marine Corps Recruit Depot Parris Island military base, and after spending some time over the phone and building our friendship, he decided that he was going to come to DC and take me out on a date. I wasn't use to any man telling me what to do. So when he told me that he was going to take me out, it shocked me, but I was also very excited so I didn't refuse. I never thought to ask him why he didn't ask me out, but he just flat out told me what was going to happen. I was an aggressive young woman, and it was an inward battle to get some instruction from a grown man concerning my actions and plans.

Nevertheless I felt so relieved because now I had a very close friend who knew about my life and knew about the things that I had been through. I liked that I had someone who enjoyed talking to me, listening to me, and was genuinely interested in getting to know me better. He respected me and didn't pressure me to have sex with him.

Shortly after he made me aware that he would take me out on a date, he drove from South Carolina and arrived in his burgundy 1997 Dodge Intrepid. I didn't have to prompt him to open any doors for me, and he allowed me to be me. We went to the movie theater to see *Deuce Bigalow: Male Gigolo*, which was by far one of the most horrible movies ever, and then we had dinner at a restaurant called Bennigan's.

We talked a lot, and it was soothing and such a relief because I was free and more comfortable with myself than I had been in the past. I enjoyed how he looked me in the eyes anytime that I spoke, and he was such a great active listener. One thing that crept me out, though, was the fact that he paid so much attention to me, and I wasn't use to that. He would just sit and stare at me. But I did the same when he wasn't looking. He was just what I had wanted and needed in my life.

We began dating in November 1999 and became an official couple on January 4, 2000. Leroy continued to court me the right way without asking for sex. He had a career and great benefits and his own car. But most importantly, he was a Christian. He had been raised in church, and although I hadn't been, pleasing God was my first priority and his. I never claimed to have it all together or to be perfect, but I was definitely trying to come close. I was trying to stay focused. Leroy was a big help, and he assisted me in reaching my goals.

We continued to work at our relationship while he was living in South Carolina and I in Maryland. It was a challenge, but we managed to make it happen. I had a hard time trusting, and that definitely got in the way of my relationship at certain points in time. But I was committed to Leroy and kept my word to remain faithful to him.

On one of his weekend visits to Maryland, he came to my apartment to visit me and offered to cook for me. Anyone who had ever known me knew that I liked to eat, and the very thing that won me over was the omelet that he cooked for me before he left for South Carolina. He also knew that I thoroughly enjoyed breakfast for dinner, so my omelet was cooked at about 8:00 p.m., and it was fantastic!

Now since he told me that he was going to take me on a date, I got him back. Payback is sometimes so sweet. I just happened to tell him on January 4, 2000, that he was going to be my man. He didn't refuse! And I'm so very glad that he didn't. He kept a smile on my face from that moment on, and on January 4, 2002, we were married at the courthouse in Upper Marlboro, Maryland. Because of his commitment to the military, we had a big wedding ceremony in April of 2002.

I am truly happy to say that we are still happily married today—and I'm still eating his omelets. God blessed me tremendously by getting my attention enough to allow the love of my life to come in and sweep (or cook) me off of my feet. I don't believe that would've happened if I kept feeling sorry for myself and dressing and acting the way that I was. It wasn't until I quieted down and stopped putting myself out there and knew who I was and what I wanted that I was able to see who God had for me. I had taken the time to set standards, and I wasn't afraid to let anyone know what they were.

# MY SURRENDER

God taught me, through his Word, to clean up my life, to be patient, and to let my husband find me. I had learned that I didn't have to let men treat me any kind of way in order to gain their respect, I didn't have to wear clothes that revealed my body in order to get their attention, and most of all, I didn't have to settle for less than what I deserve. I realized that my clothing, attitude, and standards had a lot to do with the men that I attracted. Wearing skin-tight clothing and tops that showed my belly and so forth got me just what I presented.

I got a revelation that I was the daughter of the Most High God and that I deserved the best! I wasn't completely healed, and I brought a lot of my childhood issues into my marriage, but with time, I discovered God's love for me was better than anything that I could've ever imagined. Once I discovered who I was in Christ, and the power and authority that I had as a believer, there was no turning back! I didn't know if being a Christian would benefit me, and the first thing that I did was accept Jesus into my heart and life as my personal Lord and Savior, and I waited, listened, and obeyed.

I expected things to change for the better in my life. When I submitted my life to Jesus I didn't feel any different, and as a matter of fact, I went back to some of my old ways. The more that I promised God and myself that I wouldn't do something, I did it anyway.

The very moment that I accepted Christ, I didn't get any chills up my spine, I didn't shake, cry, or anything of the sort. But I recognized that I wasn't succeeding on my own, and my hope was in Christ to help me to live for Him and to seek God first. It wasn't easy, and it didn't feel good to tell my flesh that it was going to stop clubbing, cursing, drinking, and having sex before marriage, and I had grown weary of expecting change and not wanting to put forth any effort to make a change. I couldn't walk around and quote scriptures to anyone, tell them how I understood one scripture from another, or tell a person one single Bible story.

But this is what I can tell you: God changed my entire life and let me tell you how. I didn't know how I made it through all of the mess and turmoil that I had experienced as a child—and of all of the drug addicts, pedophiles, rapists, and kidnappers that were five feet away from me at times, none of them ever touched me. Of all the times that I could've been abducted or shot up with the very same needles that I witnessed people using or hit by random gunfire on one of the many nights that my twin and I were walking home horrified in the middle of the night, God protected me!

I didn't understand the voice that calmly called out to me in the middle of the night when I wrote down and planned to commit suicide until I recognized that it was the voice of God telling me "there's more." From the time that I was five years of age, I can clearly remember all of these experiences down to the very clothes that I wore, yet I didn't lose my mind. I could've lost my mind a long time ago because of some of the things that I've seen, but God kept me! The very fact that I'm alive right now and able to share my story with you is a miracle in and of itself, and I can't attribute this great victory to anyone else but God because there was no one else there to protect me.

I spent more than fifteen years of my life feeling unworthy, unloved, unappreciated, and angry. I had so many emotional lows that I didn't understand why I had been born or why I went through all of this and why couldn't it be someone else that could handle this better than I. But now I know that I was born for such a time as this and that God has a plan for all of us. We have to be willing to surrender our lives and hearts to him and allow him to transform us one day at a time. So many people get caught up on receiving instant results and quick fixes to their problems, and sometimes it does happen that way. But we must have faith in more than just our human emotions and abilities and realize that if we could do it on our own, then it would've been done a long time ago!

I thank God for opening my eyes and allowing me to see that there is always more to life than what we think. When I decided that since I had hit my lowest point in life, where I felt that I was the one who gave myself life—therefore I had the right to take it, God chased after me and never once did he stop. I didn't hear any loud, booming voice from heaven that shouted a bunch of thus and thus, but it was the quietest most peaceful whisper that got my attention. There was no fancy language involved, and God met me right where I was and spoke to me in a way that I could understand.

I was tired of feeling guilty for the things that I had done, and I wanted peace. I was tired of being angry and not smiling because I was so focused on what wasn't right in my life, instead of what I needed to do to make things right. I learned that some struggles that we have in our lives are a result of spirits attaching themselves to our family lines and that these struggles aren't even ones that we brought on ourselves. But one of the most powerful things in life that we as human beings can learn is that though we don't have the power to make challenges and obstacles stop, we have the power to respond in such a way that God gets the glory and we are set free and have the victory over them.

I can never say it enough, this life has not been easy and things don't always go as smoothly as we may want them to go, but give God the chance to make it right! Surrender your heart, life, and your ways to him, and allow him to show you the way. This takes discipline, practice, and dedication. If we miss the mark, then we have to be strong enough to get back up and try it again.

Jesus gave his life for you and for me, and the least that we can do is give him a chance to show us the right way. It made a lot of sense to me to give Jesus the chance to make things right; to believe that he is the son of God, that he died on the cross for me, was raised from the dead, and is seated at the right hand of God; and to put my total trust in him than to live my life continuously depressed, disappointed, angry, and bitter and then die just to find out that there was something better. It was a chance that I was willing to take because I realized that I didn't have anything to lose because I had already hit my rock bottom.

# ADDICTION

An addiction is the state of being enslaved to a habit or practice or to something that is psychologically or physically habit forming (Dictionary.com). Addiction comes in many forms and is absolutely no respecter of persons. Addiction has no name, age, is not for one specific race or ethnic group, and does not turn down a willing participant. Addiction does not discriminate, and any human being can become enslaved to anything, which means that any one of us can fall short. Things such as pornography, smoking, drinking, lying, stealing, cheating, sex, food, and even exercise can become a habit-forming activity in our lives.

I thought that my parents were two strong, funny, wonderful individuals, and when they became addicted to drugs, I eventually realized that whatever they were putting into their bodies was causing the problem. As a child, I didn't know what addiction was; therefore I was so confused because I couldn't understand my parents' change in behavior. I knew that when they were just in the house, they wasn't moving slow, their eyes weren't red, and their speech wasn't slurred, but when they left for a while and then returned, all of the above were present with them.

It all started with cigarettes, and I would often hear them say that they just "can't seem to quit" and that the cigarettes "clears my mind." One thing that I observed early in life was that although they said that the cigarettes cleared their minds, their minds hardly seemed clear at all. They were always yelling, cussing, arguing, and calling each other names, and if that was a clear mind, I wanted no parts of it. I believed that they could quit because anyone who wants to do something will do it no matter the cost.

Once their problems outgrew the cigarettes, then marijuana was the next step. We'd play outside and run by or be in our room playing with our toys and smell the familiar smell of marijuana, and for a while, that was the next thing to "clear their minds."

I also learned another important concept early in life: problems will always be ever present in our lives. We don't have an iota of power to stop problems from coming our way, but we have all of the power in the world as to how we respond to the problems. One thing that I believe that my parents lacked was knowledge. Once I became an adult, I understood that a person normally doesn't do what they haven't been taught. And other times, individuals just choose to do what they do.

Growing up, I was angry, frustrated, resentful, and hurt. I didn't fully understand the intricate details of life, and I was so frustrated because no one around me understood them, and that meant no one could teach me. Although I understood that concept, it didn't take away the frustration, anger, hurt, and resentment.

A parent can teach their children to do and say all of the right things, but if they still choose to do the wrong thing, then nobody has control over that. It is my opinion that the most powerful tool that we have on planet earth is the power of choice. We as human beings have to make choices from the time that we wake up until the time that we go to sleep, and with each and every choice, there is a consequence.

My parents chose to begin their painful walk down the road of addiction by smoking cigarettes, and once that no longer gave them the escape that they needed, they moved on to marijuana. After a while, the marijuana no longer gave them the feeling of satisfaction they needed, and then came the crack cocaine and other drugs. The drug addiction became coupled with the lying addiction and the stealing addiction. They stole money and pawned furniture in order to get the drug fix that they needed.

Addiction seemed to be progressive, and once one thing doesn't satisfy the flesh, then the addict moves on to the next thing. Addiction is a vicious cycle, and when a person is addicted to something, it's hard for them to overcome without the proper confidence and help. If everyone could overcome addiction and other obstacles, then there would be no purpose for the word *help*. The word *help* means to give or provide what is necessary to accomplish a task or satisfy a need (Dictionary.com), so if we can do it alone, then this word would probably not have been created. My intent for sharing my story is to hopefully educate those who have fallen into addiction, to comfort those who have suffered on the other side of addiction, and most importantly, to prevent those who are near addiction from falling into its trap. I would at least ask any individual who has had challenges and who feels like there is something that they are enslaved to, to just think about those around you that care for and love you.

As you have already read, addiction affects your mother, father, sister, brother, children, and friends. For example, if your mother gets sick and is hospitalized, it affects you because you don't want to see her feeling bad; if your child falls while playing and scuffs his/her knee, it affects you because you don't want to see your child hurt. When you become addicted to any habit or practice, it affects those around you because your loved ones don't want to see you hurt.

There is a pain that we feel when a friend or loved one is going through something bad in their lives or when they are hurt, and it is absolutely no different to see someone that you like or love enslaved to something.

It's no fun to walk by your loved one, and they are so enslaved to an illegal substance that they won't even recognize you. There is no comfort for the wife/husband who is hurting and feeling unworthy because their spouse is enslaved to pornography.

There is no trust for the family who can't sleep at night and who is worried about how the bills will get paid or where the next meal will come from because their loved one is enslaved to gambling.

I am not an expert on addiction, and I had been addicted to looking for love in the wrong way and giving myself away as if I was some unworthy piece of trash. I was enslaved to allowing men to hide me and being too ashamed to walk in public with me or date me as a man should. But the key word here is *allowed*—we can only become enslaved to things when we allow a behavior to go uncorrected or we act on a thought. We must acknowledge our shortcomings in order to correct them. I believe that addiction starts with curiosity and then becomes progressive and compulsive, and many times, addicts aren't aware that their behavior is hurting themselves and others.

# MY PARENTS TODAY

Today, my parents are doing well. I still don't know what my parents' drug of choice was and in my opinion, it doesn't matter. Because whatever it was, it caused them to spend more time with the drugs than they did with me. I do know that they both have some unresolved issues from their own separate pasts, and I hope that one day they could get some counseling to get to the root of the issue.

My parents never married eachother and my mom has been married for 10+ years. They never reconciled or tried to make it work so that my twin and I could have a family and grow up with both parents in the same home. Nevertheless, they are each living productive lives and are able to share their stories with whomever the Lord leads them to share it with. They have been to rehabilitation programs in the past and thankfully both of my parents have given their lives to the Lord. My mom is a very hard worker and excels in every job that she has had. She was and is the most delightful and funny person and people enjoy being in her company. I can definitely get a good belly laugh when I'm around her. She loves her grandchildren and they adore her.

Today, my dad is an honorable man who loves the Lord. He is also a joy to be around because he is funny and he too is a hardworking man. I love them dearly and although it was not my preferred way of learning, they taught me some very valuable lessons!

# ELEVEN WAYS TO AVOID ADDICTION

## 1. BE HONEST WITH YOURSELF AND OTHERS

Being honest with yourself and knowing what you like and dislike, what irritates you and what puts a smile on your face, is a great reflection of how others will treat and respect you. When people ask you to do something and you agree to do it knowing that you really don't want to do it is not being honest with yourself. If someone asks your opinion and you know that you didn't give them the honest answer, then you're not being honest with yourself.

It is perfectly fine to tell your friend the truth when she tries on a dress that is three sizes too small and you think that she looks horrible in it, that the dress doesn't compliment her. If you don't like it when people say certain things to you, it is okay to make them aware of it. It is always best to express how you feel about something and stand firm on what you believe in. If you're wrong about something, it is okay to be honest and admit that you were wrong.

A major part of how other people will treat you is being honest with yourself. If other people see you saying one thing and living another, then it's hard for them to give you the respect that you feel that you deserve. We must be honest with how we feel about ourselves and what we think of ourselves.

I spent more than fifteen years of my life feeling ugly, unworthy, stupid, sad, and like there was absolutely no one in the world who loved me and wanted me around. Yet I was not very honest with myself because I walked around as if everything was okay and I acted like I was superwoman and could handle any and everything.

I didn't look people in the eye when I spoke to them because I was ashamed of who I was. I was weak, and I held all of my feelings inside because I wasn't honest enough to share with anyone and tell them how I really felt. I wanted to sit my parents down and tell them how much their actions and/or words hurt me to the core and how their actions made me feel totally opposite of how I should have felt as a little girl and even as an adult.

I have been married for almost eleven years now, and I have brought so many of those negative feelings into my marriage and made my husband pay for the mistakes that my parents made. In the beginning, I wasn't honest with him about how I felt because I wasn't honest with myself. For years, I told myself that I was fine and I was the one holding it down for everyone else and I didn't need any help. But since we're being honest here, I needed any and all of the help that I could get.

I can even go so far as to say that while writing this book, it took me so long to share my story because I wanted to fancy it up and tell the world my story but not tell it exactly how it happened for fear of people judging me or my family. But finally after much praying and fighting with myself, I decided that the truth always prevails.

Honesty is not a characteristic that society upholds right now. There are politicians who lie, people enter in contracts with one another and don't keep their end of the agreement, and marriages are broken and ended more easily than ever because of dishonesty. I have stepped out and have taken this opportunity to share with you all that; no matter the judgment from people or the consequences that come with any and every choice that we make, the truth is always the best and only option.

## 2.  FIND YOUR GIFTS AND TALENTS

Is there something that you really enjoy doing? What are your gifts and talents? There are many things on earth that we can possibly do for fun, as a job, career, or hobby. But what is it that you can do naturally that blesses other people? Gifts come in many different areas, and each and every individual has their own unique gift. This means that even if you have fifty people working in a grocery store, and some have the same titles and daily duties, each person's gift is unique.

Once we find out what our gifts are, then we are more likely to spend time maturing our gifts and more time putting our gifts to work, and it could possibly leave less time to think about how difficult our life or situation may be. Finding out what you were born to do and then stepping over into your purpose is fulfilling and brings you satisfaction. Oftentimes, we make poor choices and become stagnant or inactive, sluggish, or dull, and we just wander around aimlessly believing that life "is what it is." Instead, we should be focused on knowing who we are and what it is that we enjoy doing, and that in return will bless someone else's life.

When we have so much time on our hands, we tend to become stagnant and start to complain about our situation instead of changing it. I don't know about you, but I get total satisfaction when I use my gifts and then it turns right around and causes someone else to change their life for the better. I believe that this very book that you're reading right now will cause someone to put down the weed, alcohol, the pornography, discontinue lying, gambling, and stealing and begin to go after their gift so that someone else can benefit from it.

I'm a firm believer that our gifts aren't for us. A gift is defined as something given voluntarily without payment in return or simply the act of giving. Most times while we're giving, we aren't focused on our own desires and needs or wants. So spend time finding out what your gift is, and then spend even more time giving it away by being a blessing to someone. Your gift could be to wait tables, seat people, greet people at Walmart, be a police officer, camera man/woman, work for sales, collections, customer service, mechanic, and so much more. So on purpose, find out what it is that you are gifted at, then go out and give to someone else. Remember that your gift is not for you; it's for someone else, and when you give it away, you get blessed in return.

## 3. SET GOALS

Once you find out what your gift is you can then begin to plan how to use your gift. Write your short- and long-term goals down, and once they are reached, cross them out and write some more. This keeps our hope up and keeps us moving forward to accomplish something. Setting goals and accomplishing those keeps us busy and gives us less time to worry about the negative things.

Our goals should never be limited, and we should always make accomplishing them realistic. We should not set a goal to become an astronaut in five days or obtain a college degree in six months when we have never been to college. Setting unrealistic timeframes to accomplish your goals will cause you to become frustrated and give up. Setting short-term goals give you something to work toward and are usually accomplished in a short period of time. The timeframe for our short-term goals to be accomplished is usually anywhere from one day to a few months. Long term goals tend to be the goals that mean more to us, and they also are more difficult to achieve because we get distracted and discouraged. Long-term goals take more time to accomplish but are set to be accomplished from one year to ten years.

Some examples of short-term goals are passing a test, rearranging a room in your home, or enrolling in college (if you're a senior in high school). Some examples of long-term goals are obtaining a college degree if you've just graduated from high school, purchasing your dream home in five years, or planning a wedding in two years. These types of goals keep us focused and keep us looking forward to the end result. Once we've reached these goals, we should pull out the tablet that we wrote them down on and cross them off of our list. We should also celebrate with the accomplishing of each individual goal and then set new goals to replace the ones that have already been accomplished.

## 4. REDUCE NEGATIVE STRESS

In case you didn't know, you can't eliminate stress from your life. To be honest, I've learned that I don't want to totally eliminate stress from life. I know you may be wondering why, and I'll be sure to answer that question later. But we *can* eliminate our negative reaction to stress.

In all that I've gone through in my life, I couldn't see how any of it would have helped me to become the woman that I am today and I couldn't see how it could have help me or anyone else for that matter. But when I got into high school, I started to program myself to see the positive in anything. No matter how hard it seems and how much you struggle to maintain your sanity, there is always a positive in everything, and there is always a lesson to be learned when you go through anything.

Speaking and thinking positive helps us to reduce negative stress in our lives. When we focus on the positive and how we are going to overcome the obstacles in our lives, then we reduce the negative thoughts and effects of stress. This takes practice and time because we all know that it is hard to focus on the positive when we're in the midst of a storm.

Imagine yourself standing outside in the middle of a football field during a bad thunderstorm, where it is lightning, thundering, the wind is blowing, and it is raining so hard that you can't see your hand in front of your face. Wouldn't it be pretty hard to stand there and think rationally? Some people would automatically begin to run, not knowing what's in front of them or which direction they are headed.

Many times this is exactly what is going on in some people's lives. They are being laid off from work, family members are calling them and depending on them to fix everyone else's problems, bills are stacking up and money is not coming in, their children are acting out and they don't understand why. Some people just take off running and don't think rationally, and they end up turning to drugs, alcohol, pornography, and other harmful habit- forming things because they don't know how to properly handle stress. They turn to these negative things to pacify the stress, and the result of that is that they eventually become enslaved to those things.

Pacifying stress can become progressive and compulsive because stress is a normal part of life, and not understanding how to deal with it causes people to self-medicate and think that these other things will cause their problems to go away when in reality, it harms the mind and/or body.

There are positive stressors, such as planning a wedding, studying for your last exam before you finish a class, and deciding what kind and color of car to purchase. In my opinion, positive stress is needed and gives you a sense of victory and accomplishment because you have some sort of control over the end result. Speaking positive, believing the positive, and focusing on the positive will help you reduce the negative stress in your life.

## 5.   HANDLE NEGATIVE THOUGHTS IMMEDIATELY

Quite often, when obstacles arise, we don't think sensibly in regard to how we overcome the obstacle. Some people are irrational and look for a quick pacifier that makes them feel better, instead of getting to the root of the problem. Our number 1 mistake that we make when trying to deal with stress and overcome obstacles is that when the irrational thoughts arise, we sleep on them and give ourselves too much time to think about them. I believe that it is okay for us to think on how we can overcome obstacles, but when you recognize that a thought is unhealthy, then its best to dismiss it immediately.

Think about this one carefully: when you have an argument with your spouse and you all don't talk about it and you lie down at night and go to sleep with the intention of discussing the issue in the morning, what happens next? You lie down and let the problem sit, and some of us are even aggravated and can't sleep well that night, and when you wake up in the morning, you are still aggravated and oftentimes can't effectively resolve the issue. Another way to think of this is when you put a pot roast in a slow cooker, and you season the meat with different seasonings and set the timer. The pot slowly heats up, and the meat begins to cook. The seasonings set in and make the meat tender and break it down to where it begins to separate. And by the time the designated time is up, the meat is no longer together and in one piece because for four, eight, or ten hours, it has stewed.

The same thing occurs when negative thoughts arise, and we don't kick them out of our thought process immediately. The negative thoughts stew for hours, and just like the meat, it would be hard to put the pot roast back together in its original state. We then have all of these pieces of thoughts in our heads and end up having more than one problem when we go to resolve the initial problem. We end up with more than one problem because we start thinking about old stuff that seems similar to the current problem, and things get blown out of proportion.

One thing that I've learned to do, whether it seems crazy or not, is I would speak to the negative thought out loud. I'd tell myself, "I will not allow this to be an option." We have to train ourselves to think positively and get rid of the negative thoughts as soon as they arise. We do have control over what we do with our thoughts, and we can either keep them or get rid of them.

## 6.   BE MINDFUL OF WHO YOU HANG AROUND

Surround yourself with people who are positive thinkers and speakers and who share some of the same goals that you have. If you try to reduce the negative stress and its negative effects, then surrounding yourself with people who complain and who think and talk negatively will more than likely cause you to do the same.

A lot of times, the people that you associate with or spend the bulk of your time with can be a great influence on you. The people that you hang around can also stop your blessings because they can influence your thinking and cause you to see the negative in everything, and all the while, you're missing the good thing that's right in front of you. Whenever you focus the bulk of your time and attention on the negative aspects of anything, it creates negative stress, and you spend the majority of your time complaining.

It is also a good idea to surround yourself with people who share some of the same interests that you do and have some of the same short- and long-term goals that you have. Therefore, you can become accountable to someone else, you all can work together to accomplish your goals, and you can be there to encourage each other to accomplish your goals.

Surrounding yourself with people who have things in common gives you the opportunity to build genuine relationships and talk about things with someone who understands what you might be going through. Iron sharpens iron, and we should always be mindful of who we have around us. We should desire and then find those who will speak the truth to us in love and not be afraid to cry when we cry or laugh when we laugh. We don't need people around us who will be jealous when something good happens to us, and we need those people who will be there to hug us, listen to us, and help us to heal when there is something traumatic that has occurred in our lives or when we're simply having a rough day.

Another great point to think about when choosing your friends is to know their character, and before calling someone your friend, you need to watch them. And when I say watch them, I mean sit back and physically watch them and how they react to people, how they respond to others and how they speak. Do they talk negatively about situations, or do they speak positively? Do they gossip and can't seem to keep anybody else's news to themselves? It is important to watch a person and get to know their character because if you see them talking about people, gossiping, or getting upset about everything, then rest assured that if they are doing that with other people, they will do the same for you. I'm not saying to avoid people who have character flaws like the ones that I've just written, and if you choose to call them "friend," then it is your choice. I do believe that we have purposes in life and that we have assignments in life. I believe that we come into other people's lives to help them to grow, and then some people come into our lives to help us to grow in a certain area.

It is important to choose people that will help you to grow. For example, if you get into a disagreement with someone, then you call a friend or family member to get some advice or just to vent, and the first thing that family member or friend tells you is, "Just cuss them out" or "I would slap him/her the first chance that I get" or "I would drop them like a bad habit," then that's probably not the person that you should go to in order to get advice or help from. Now having someone who says, "Well, maybe they didn't mean it that way" or "They could've been having a bad day and didn't mean to speak to you that way" would cause you to calm down and think the situation through and help you to respond positively instead of reacting negatively.

Quite a bit of the conflicts that we get involved in are miscommunications or misunderstandings. We are all different, and we give and receive information differently. It is important to have people around us who understand this concept so that they can help us on the days that are a challenge to us. Each and every day, we have the opportunity to grow or not grow, and having quality people around you should be a high priority in your life. A friendship should not be one sided and should not be developed to where one person is manipulated and only one person gets something out of the relationship. Friendships should be taken seriously and should be valued.

## 7.   BE ACCOUNTABLE.

If you begin to notice that you are becoming addicted to a habit or that you feel like you have to depend on a certain person, substance, or action in order for you to feel good, then it is possible that you may be getting closer to becoming an addict. We'll discuss some warning signs of addiction later.

This point ties directly with being mindful of who you surround yourself with because on those days that are more challenging, it helps if you can call up a friend or family member who speaks positively and think positively. For me personally, I begin to think more clearly and rationalize better when I hear myself telling one of my friends or family members what my struggle is and then ask for ideas on how to resolve my issue. A lot of our stress can be minimized if we can sit down or call someone else and say out loud whatever it is that we are struggling with.

In order to change something and grow, we have to be able to acknowledge that there is a problem. Acknowledging a problem is not enough, so we must come up with a plan to resolve the issue. And I'll even go so far as to say that acknowledgment is not even the last step to being accountable for what we do. Once we acknowledge that there is a problem, and we come up with some ideas on how to resolve the problem, then we must take action. We can recognize problems all day long, but a part of being accountable for our actions is to take action.

Move forward and take the appropriate action to resolving conflict, or get to the root of the stress in your life by identifying the problem and taking steps to make it right. For example, when you have an argument with someone and you disagree about something, instead of jumping on some social media website to character-bash the person or sending them a text message that can be interpreted all kinds of ways, be accountable and make it right.

One way to make it right is to go to the person directly and say, "Hey, what you said hurt my feelings" or "I felt very disrespected when you did that." Sometimes, the person will be willing to say, "I really didn't mean it that way," or simply say, "I'm sorry for that." Sometimes we get so into our feelings, and we feel strongly about certain topics that we just start flying off of the handle or speaking harshly or openly and not consider who our audience is. And we genuinely do offend the listener, although it wasn't our intention.

Another example is if you know that there is negative stress in your life, then you owe it to yourself to be honest about what or who the thing or person is that stresses you. If you know that when you encounter this person or thing it causes you to pick up a cigarette to "calm your nerves" or run out and get a case of beer to help you to "unwind" then, being accountable means that you get to the source of what the stressor is and call a friend, family member, or support group and say, "This particular situation is stressing me out and is causing me to want to get high." Hopefully, the people around you will say, "Instead of getting high, or smoking a cigarette, why don't we go to the mall or go for a walk and talk about it."

Resolving the issue may take more than a walk in the park or a trip to the mall, and so having people around you that can give you fresh and new ideas is so very important and is definitely a part of us being accountable for our actions. Fear and pride can paralyze us and keep us from growing and obtaining total victory in our lives. Being accountable is to stop self-medicating our issues or pacifying our hurt and pain. It is just acknowledging that there is an issue, confronting the issue by saying it out loud, pushing fear and pride aside, asking someone for help, and then just stepping out on faith and simply making it right.

## 8. EXERCISE SELF-CONTROL.

Now that we've learned that we must learn to know ourselves, be honest with ourselves and others, find out what our gifts and talents are, set short- and long-term goals, reduce negative stress, handle negative thoughts as soon as they arise, be mindful of who you hang around, and be accountable to someone else, we can focus on our responses or reactions to circumstances.

When it comes to overcoming obstacles, it can be frustrating, easy, stressful, or difficult. Since we've learned that we can't stop problems from coming our way, it's now time to recognize that we can control how we allow those problems to affect us and those around us. In all that we do, we have to acknowledge that there are decisions to be made and consequences of how we respond or react. Self-control is the control or restraint of oneself or one's actions, feelings, etc. (Dictionary.com). This means that we can choose how we handle circumstances, and we can choose how to speak to people, choose to run from issues or get to the root of them and solve them. When you get into a confrontation with someone, and you want to slap some sense into them, take a moment and exercise some self-control and think about your consequences before you react.

When exercising or practicing self-control, you either choose to react or respond. To *react* is to act in response to another person, stimulus, etc. (*Collins World English Dictionary*) or to act in opposition, as against some force (Dictionary.com). To *respond* is to reply or answer in words or to react favorably (dictionary. com). Based on these definitions, it is my belief that it takes no effort or thought to react to something, and most times, it is easier to act in opposition.

But we must learn to choose and then practice reacting favorably. This normally doesn't happen on the first try and may never be done 100 percent of the time, and I can tell you from experience that I have not completely mastered this. Since I've shared the importance of being honest with yourself and others, as long as I'm on this earth, I won't get this right 100 percent of the time because a part of being human is that we are imperfect. But I can proudly say that today I am much better at reacting favorably than I use to be.

Back in the day, I had a major problem with reacting. Because I was hurting, I didn't care how I said things, and I didn't care who it hurt. I described it as "telling it like it is," with no regard for my listening audience. I felt like other people were going to hurt one way or another, so I said whatever I wanted to say. As I matured, I began to practice responding and practicing how to control myself, and I realized that I wasn't accomplishing anything by causing others to hurt because I was hurting. In the end, my hurt had not gone away.

No one else can force you to react or respond, but practice controlling and restraining yourself by controlling and restraining your actions and feelings. Be sure not to act on your feelings because our feelings tend to change from circumstance to circumstance. We sometimes wake up "feeling" bad or "feeling" like our day is going to be hectic or busy, and then before we think things through, we walk around with a chip on our shoulder and aggravated and reacting all day. Please avoid relying on your *feelings* when practicing self-control, and take time to train your heart by putting positive things before your eyes and in your ears, and it'll be much easier to respond instead of react.

## 9.   KNOW THAT YOU ARE NOT ALONE.

During my entire childhood, I walked around thinking that no one loved me, or understood me. Even though I had a twin sister right by my side, and we experienced things together, I felt like she couldn't fully understand me and I couldn't fully understand her. I struggled with feelings of unworthiness, hurt, pain, anger, resentment, and feeling unwanted by anyone. Things weren't the way that I wanted them to be or the way that I thought that they should be, so I became angry, and most times, I held it all in.

For years I felt like I couldn't talk to anyone because I assumed that no one was going to understand anyway. I felt like people had given up on me and that I was a waste of flesh. I looked around me, and everyone else's life seemed to be together and in one piece. The other kids at school seemed happy and as if their households were intact. I felt like they tortured me so much because I was the only one who was going through things. When in actuality, they talked about me, hit me, threw things at me, and told my business to anyone who would listen because they too were hurting and could possibly have been going through the same situation that I was. After all, they lived in the same neighborhood, and some of my family hung out with their families. It took me a long time to realize that I wasn't the only one with issues and I never would be.

I spent many nights lying in bed awake because I didn't open up to someone. I was embarrassed because of the choices that my parents made and that I was stuck with their decisions until I was mature enough to move out and make my own. I was ashamed to look people in the eyes because of a fear that they might recognize my pain and cause me to open up and talk about it. I was so angry because I kept it all in, and I wouldn't even crack a smile because I was afraid to open up and let people see the gifts and talents that I had for fear that they may want to spend more time with me and get to know me and then more of me would be exposed. I wouldn't sit up straight or walk straight, and I made every attempt to shrink away from everyone because I was deceived into thinking that no one would understand or relate to me.

It is not conducive to one's health and well-being to try and fight battles on our own or conquer things on our own. Going through life alone is never the best option because there is always someone who can relate to you, understand you, or just sympathize with you and be there to hold your hand and give you a fresh new idea. We must understand the importance of relationships and value the relationships that we build, and then retain those relationships by being transparent. It is okay to allow someone else to see you hurt or to see you happy.

Not everyone will fully understand you or what you're struggling with, nor will they have good intentions in helping you to overcome your struggles. Some people do take advantage of others or see someone's kindness as a weakness, but that is where your self-control comes into play. Once you recognize those people who aren't good to have around you, then kindly dismiss them from your life. It is okay to go to them and tell them why you don't think they are helping you to grow, and if you all decide to remain in each other's company, then continue to grow and move on. If you decide to discontinue your relationship, then grow and move on.

Because I felt so alone for so many years, when true love showed up, I didn't even recognize and appreciate it. When I allowed Jesus into my heart and accepted him as my personal Lord and Savior, I still didn't get it right away. I still carried on with some of the same feelings and behaviors, and through practicing self- control, I began to practice receiving true and unconditional love. Before accepting Jesus into my heart I had never heard of anyone who had loved me, no matter how I looked, what I said or did, or how many times I messed up. But then I began to open up and be honest with myself, and I admitted that I couldn't handle all of life's problems alone.

My feelings had overtaken me and had kept me so bottled up that I couldn't share my gifts and talents with anyone else. I surrendered, and I began to see what true and unconditional love was like and that I didn't have to pretend to be someone different in order to receive it, I didn't have to put on an act for it, I didn't have to beg for it, I didn't have to work for it, and most importantly, I didn't have to be perfect for it. I didn't have to stop cussing or having sex out of wedlock or stop drinking in order to receive this unconditional love.

The point that I'm trying to make is that I didn't have to clean everything up in my life before coming to Jesus, but over time I remained open and allowed him to clean me up. I accepted his love, and I allowed it over time to cleanse me, repair my heart, renew my mind, and over time, I had no desire to cuss someone out when they offended me, I had no desire to give myself away to a man to make me feel better about myself, I had no desire to pick up a glass of alcohol to pacify my problems, and I recognized that I'm human and would never get everything right 100 percent of the time.

The best thing of all about this unconditional love is that it's already paid for. How good would it feel if somebody gave you something that caused you to look better, feel better, and sound better and then told you that it was free of charge? Women, don't you love that new pair of shoes and how they make your feet look so nice and how they make an outfit just stand out when you wear it? Men, don't you love how that suit makes you feel like you're somebody of importance and makes you stand up taller and walk differently? Well, there is absolutely no difference in God's love! When we understand and accept it, it will make you feel brand new and just right!

Once I understood that Jesus had already been beaten, bruised, spit on, and had given his life for me, then I no longer had to work so hard for another man to love me. It's amazing how some people say that they love you, and as soon as you do something that they don't like, then oops! They won't love you anymore like they use to or like they said that they did.

With the unconditional love from God, we can mess up, and may have messed up, more times that we can count, yet he still loves us. He may not be pleased with what we've done, but his love never changes and never fails, and we can come back to him as many times as we need to in order to get another chance to get it right. And all that it takes is acknowledging that we've missed it and turning in the opposite direction and asking him to forgive us and teach us how to get it right.

Don't you like free stuff ? I love it when I go to the grocery store and they hand out samples of food and you get to try it before you buy it. Just to create some balance here, not everything that is free is good or right for you. The people that are handing out the food don't pick out who they think might qualify to taste the food; they just hand it out freely. Well, God's love is just about the same. He's standing and hoping that he will get your attention and cause you to walk up to him with an open mind and heart and a desire to try what he is offering you.

But he doesn't hand us a small sample of his love and say, "There's more on aisle 6 if you want to buy it." He hands us a complete love package and says, "You don't have to pay for it. Take it. It's all yours," and we can choose to accept it or not. His package does not promise us a problem-free life, just like the grocery store worker doesn't promise you that the food sample won't upset your stomach or give you a bad taste in your mouth. But what God's package does promise us is a life of victory and overcoming obstacles, freedom from fear, anger, and lying. It also promises us that we have access to infinite knowledge, growth, healing, wealth, riches, prosperity, and a life of sharing his love with others.

Remember that you are never alone. There is always someone else going through the same thing that you are experiencing or something similar. I can even go so far as to say that there is always someone going through something worse than you and would love to trade places with you. So reach out and get to know people because we will all experience hurt at some point in our lives, and we can let it cripple us or cause us to move forward. I have shared my hurt and my struggles with you all in hopes that you will know that you are not alone.

## 10.   BE MINDFUL OF YOUR WORDS .

I've said it more than once, and I'm sure it won't be the last time that I'll say it. That silly little childhood song that says "Sticks and stones may break my bones, but words will never hurt me" is so very far from the truth. If no one has ever told you that words hurt, let me be the first.

I spent so many years believing the negative words that kids and my mom used toward me. It was never the spankings that made me feel sad and unwanted. It was the words that tore my life apart and tore down my self-esteem. It was the words that I had to hear from kids at school that caused me to feel hurt, embarrassed, and angry, and when I went home, all that I longed for were three words. Instead, I heard "Don't take that from nobody. Cuss them out" and "So what? Let them talk."

Negative words had become a normal part of my life, and they bounced back and forth in my head and echoed in the night and kept me from enjoying a peaceful night's sleep. Words kept me from smiling and kept me from exploring life. Words discouraged me and caused fear to creep up and put me in a choke hold.

Words make an impression on the heart, whether they are positive words or negative. Especially as a child, words help them to form a self-image, and they soak your words up like a sponge. Children are clean slates, and we, by example, teach them how to be. Children start out by repeating what they hear those around them say, even when they don't know the meaning of the words. Children are listening, even when we don't think that they are.

As a child, I understood way more than the adults around could've imagined. I began to memorize words. My grandma's favorite line when I asked her what a word meant was to "look it up," and I did just that. As a child, words fascinated me, and even as an adult, I love to learn new words and spend time developing my vocabulary. I enjoy word games and word searches because words are in everything.

Words can encourage or discourage, and learning when and how we should use them can encourage yourself and others or it will do just the opposite. To add some balance to this, not everyone responds to words the same, and it is easier for some people to say "That's not me" or "Whatever" and just dismiss negative words. Negative words crippled me, and it was hard to just let them roll off of my back. If there was more of a balance in my life while growing up, then I would have probably felt differently about words and the use of them.

Speaking positive words uplifts people and gives them hope. Positive speaking causes positive thinking, and we should always stop and think before we open up our mouths and speak about any subject or to anyone. As I grew older, I used words to encourage myself and to reverse all of the negative words that had paralyzed and desensitized me.

Words caused my original innocence to be broken. I thought that negative speaking was a normal part of life, and as a child, I didn't get to experience the feeling of walking with my head up and my chest out because I felt like I could do anything. I had many gifts and talents, but because I was never told that I could be anything that I wanted to be, I didn't believe that I could.

As I mentioned before, I only wanted to hear three words when I came home. During the school days, I constantly heard that I was stupid, black, skinny, ugly, dumb, and never going to amount to anything. The kids would pull my long hair, kick me, hit me, push me, and were constantly speaking negatively to and about me. And when I got home, there was no one to remedy this negative action. Most times, there was no one home when I got home to listen to me and ask how my day went. There was no one to hug me, help me, and give me ideas on how to fix it. My father wasn't around, and whenever my mother was around, she was cussing, fussing, yelling, and calling names.

I'm sure by now you're wondering what the three words were that I not only wanted to hear, but needed to hear. I simply needed my mom, grandma, or someone to say "It's not true." A lot of people may need to hear "I love you," but I just needed someone to lay some foundation and help me to believe that the cruelty that I dealt with outside of my home was not the way that life should be. Instead, when I got home, there was no one to tell me that cruelty, hurt, pain, and anger was not normal and that I was worth something.

Be very mindful of how you say things, and work hard at ridding your life and your children's lives of negative speaking. Be sure to spend quality time with them, listen to them, and cast negative thoughts away as soon as you think them or are made aware of them. Children will tell you exactly how they feel—unfiltered. And it is our duty to help them to know when and how to speak and how important it is to understand what they are saying and that their words will encourage or discourage. Spend time encouraging yourself and others by replacing your negative words with positive ones and on purpose, only speaking what will benefit and uplift yourself and others.

## 11. BE MADE WHOLE.

Wherever you might be right now, emotionally, physically, mentally, or spiritually, I implore you to be mindful of what you say and do. Be an example for someone! The very words that you use can build someone up and help them to recognize their gifts and talents and to use them to encourage others, or they can tear someone down and paralyze them, which in turns hurts someone else, because our gifts and talents are not for us.

It is never too late, and we must make a conscious decision to know better and then to do better. I carried so much baggage into my adult life, then into my marriage, and finally into motherhood because I wasn't whole. But now I walk with my head up, I smile because I have true love and joy, and I look people in the eye because I'm no longer ashamed of where I've come from and what I've been through.

Of all of the minute things in my life that I can take credit for, my being made whole is not one of them. I had experienced being scared beyond imagination—being alone in the middle of the night, with my twin and I walking the streets trying to get home, or being huddled up in a dark and foreign room of some crack house, waiting on my mother to return me to something more familiar. I had been into wanting to take my own life, struggling to pay bills while going to school, taking on way too much responsibility while trying to find myself, feeling like there was no more hope and that my life was a waste. I was angry, resentful, sad, and depressed, but God, through Jesus Christ, stepped in and taught me the value of life and that there was true love available to me and that it wasn't far away.

I can't attribute to anyone but God my peace, my love, my joy, that pleasant and gentle voice in the middle of the night that told me, "There's more," and the fact that I was never molested or abducted or I was never stuck with any of the many drug needles that I saw. He protected me when there were armed men behind bushes on either side of the street I was walking down and when my mom had a gun pressed to the side of her head in an elevator. He taught me how to love unconditionally and how to forgive.

He taught me that forgiveness was healthy and was for me and others. He taught me how to stand up for what I believe in and not back down because of who I used to be. He taught me to hold my head up high and that what I've done in the past doesn't define who I am today.

I couldn't accept true love before I knew who he was, and I couldn't accept love from my own husband because I was so torn down and didn't understand what true love really was. I'm 100 percent convinced that until you find true love, you can't love yourself or anyone else, and I'm eternally grateful that God loved me enough to send his only begotten Son so that I could experience this wholeness and help someone else to realize that if we alone could make ourselves whole, then it would've been done a long time ago. We cannot fight the battle alone, and we are not alone!

I praise God that I'm no longer confused or deceived, but my heart knows the truth, and I'll never go back. I have a wonderful husband of almost eleven years, a beautiful nine-year- old daughter, a better relationship with my parents, an awesome twin sister, and a great host of other family members who are supportive and loving.

The one most important thing that I am eternally grateful for is that I have my mind. Of all of the things that I have seen, and all of the things that I have done and gone through, I could've lost my mind. But God! I didn't understand it until I came into relationship with him, that he made me strong and that I went through those things for a reason. I am grateful that he has used me to be an example to others.

In my opinion, my childhood wasn't as pleasant or as easy as someone else's may have been, but I can stand tall today because

I am whole. And God has restored the time for me. He has me in the state that I was supposed to be in a long time ago. I find and focus on the positive in any situation. I can't stop smiling—I have a peace inside of me that I don't fully understand and so much more because God has brought me back to my original state.

It was never God's plan for us to be confused, sad, resentful, unhappy, depressed, hurt physically, emotionally, or mentally, or sick, because he has a plan for you and for me, and we can never fulfill his plan for us if we are so stuck on ourselves and consumed with fixing our own issues. He used my husband to help heal my heart and to get over past hurts and to show me that there is a man on earth who could respect me, not take advantage of or be ashamed of me, and how to love me just as he does. He blessed me with someone that I can hold, talk to, vent to, cry and heal with.

I am not perfect, and since I am human, I still have negative thoughts that enter my mind and challenges that I deal with, but now I overcome them with a different mindset. I look for something positive in everything, and I identify the lesson in everything. I am not ashamed to lift my hands, open my mouth, and give God praise for all that he has done for me, no matter where I am. Now I sing, dance, jump, run, and shout with joy because I am no longer bound by negative thoughts; they no longer cause me to feel unworthy and sad. I am whole, and I am no longer angry or resentful because I'm overflowing with peace and happiness.

I blamed my parents for not knowing better and doing better, and that caused me to harbor anger and pain, which led to me suffering from depression for more that fifteen years. But when God made me whole, I forgave them for not making better choices and for forcing me into a lifestyle that I never asked for. God brought me through it.

For those who have been abused, molested, abducted, or enslaved to anything that is habit-forming, give it to God, and don't be afraid to talk about it, cry about it, forgive, trust, and love unconditionally because none of us know when our time on this earth is over, and you never know who your healing is for.

Once you've been made whole and you begin to overflow in the things of God, you can pour his love into someone else's life. Life is more fulfilling when you live it filled with joy and peace that no man can take away from you. Don't depend on another human being to make you whole because human beings are, and will always be, imperfect. Remember that your healing, peace, joy, restoration, gifts, and talents are not for you!

# DAILY CONFESSION

Whenever you are challenged with negative thoughts and you find yourself struggling with low self-esteem because of what people have said to you, or when you just feel less than victorious, you sometimes have to encourage yourself. Here is a confession similar to the one that I spoke out loud daily until I believed in my own heart that I was fearfully and wonderfully made and until I knew that I was just the opposite of the words that had been spoken to me.

I am beautiful, and God made me this way. I love me just the way that I am. I am intelligent, and I know that I will live up to my full potential. Despite what anyone says to me today, I decide to hold my head up and believe the best in myself. I am wise beyond my years, and I make wise decisions.

I love myself and I recognize that at least one other person on earth loves me. Whatever I am unhappy with concerning myself, I change it because I decided to change it and not because someone doesn't approve of it. No human being on this earth has a heaven or a hell to put me in; therefore, their negative words won't cause me to walk around ashamed, with my head down or feeling sorry for myself.

On this day, I choose to stand erect and continue to move forward in accomplishing my goals, and no one will stop me from doing that. I have a great mind and a great memory, and I will use my gifts and talents to benefit someone else. I am worth more than the finest jewel, car, or house, and I treat myself as such. I get rid of negative thoughts immediately, and I choose to believe the opposite of them. I am confident, I am strong, I am beautiful, I am precious, I am gifted and talented, and I am loved.

My positive thoughts of myself will not change with circumstances, and I will stand up for myself. God made me beautiful and nobody can change my mind. I love me, and at least one other person does too because God gave me life and knows my beginning through my end! He formed and knew me before the foundation of the world, and therefore he knows me better than I know myself. I am more than a conqueror, and I can do all things through Christ who strengthens me!

# THE NARROW PATH

Have you ever wondered why you've tried so many things to satisfy yourself? And when that thing doesn't work, you move on to something else. Some go from man to man, drug to drug, woman to woman, school to school, church to church, friend to friend and expecting to become satisfied. I went from drink to drink and went from one man to the other in search of true love but had to continue to go back for more. I spent so much time feeling guilty after each drink and each sexual encounter, and I finally decided to just give up. I didn't know much about giving my life to Christ, but at least one special person in my life took time to pray with and for me and invited me to church where I learned that the only way that I would be satisfied, was to give my life to Jesus.

Life has not been perfect for me, even after giving my life to Christ, but it sure is better than it used to be. I stopped giving myself so many options and learned that there is only one way to total satisfaction. I still can't teach a whole list of Bible stories, but I can share with and show you what God and only God has done for me! I've been through a lot, and I'm sure that everyone has his/her own story of struggle and triumph.

It wasn't until I surrendered all of my ways, flaws, and my whole heart to God that I knew that I would overcome any and every obstacle that came my way. The only way that we can come into this victorious relationship with God is to confess with your mouth and believe in your heart that Jesus died for your sins and rose again with all power in his hands and that once and for all he gave his life for you!

Imagine this: every time that you told a lie, broke a law, or did something that was just ethically wrong, there was a punishment for it. Since there is no level of sin or lying, there is a charge for each and every wrongdoing, whether it was considered major or minor. Some of the wrongdoings could even lead to your life being ended. So you called up all of your friends or family members and asked if anyone could take the punishment for you, but all replied, "I didn't do it, so why should I take the punishment for it?" Wouldn't it feel good to have someone to step up and say, "Although I didn't commit the offense, I'll take the punishment for you."

Well, Jesus did just that! He stepped in and took on the punishment for all of mankind, one time, so that we didn't have to do it. He was beaten, bruised, spit on, and ridiculed, and through it all he never complained, and most importantly, he didn't change his mind.

Jesus is the only way to get into relationship with God. Jesus is the narrow path, so choose to take the narrow path and come to him as you are. You don't have to get everything right first—just allow him to help you to clean up your life. None of us can do it alone! I am whole today only because of my relationship with God, through Jesus. I decided to take the narrow path, and I give God all of the glory, honor, and praise because he and he alone saved me. He never gave up on me, and he won't give up on you! If you desire to have a relationship with God, confess the following prayer of salvation and believe it in your heart, and you will be saved.

Dear God in heaven, I come to you in the name of Jesus and I acknowledge that I have sinned before you and I ask for your forgiveness.

Romans 10:9–10 says, "That if thou shalt confess with thy mouth the Lord Jesus, and shalt believe in thine heart that God hath raised him from the dead, thou shalt be saved. For with the heart man believeth unto righteousness; and with the mouth confession is made unto salvation."

Therefore, I believe in my heart that Jesus is the Son of God and for my sins he died on the cross at Calvary and was raised again so that I may have eternal life. I believe in my heart and confess with my mouth that Jesus is the Son of God. Jesus, come into my heart as my personal Lord and Savior and save me now. Thank you for saving me and forgiving me. Amen.

Congratulations! You are now born again. You may not see an immediate change, or as I've stated before, you may not feel a spooky jooky feeling. But know that God is here, Jesus is alive, and that you can overcome any obstacle! You have the victory! You can be better than you are right now. Just take your spiritual growth one day at a time. Don't give up on God because he will never give up on you! Get connected with a church that takes the time to teach you the Word of God so that you can be taught how to walk out this journey and stay on the narrow path.

# AFTERWORD

You can continue to wallow in depression, negativity, sorrow, anger, resentment, hatred, or you can rise up and take control of your feelings and be joy filled, honest, trusting, trustworthy, and victorious over any situation in your life. You can choose to hang with people who constantly complain, talk negative, and are stagnant themselves, or you can choose to become iron. Sharpen iron by linking up with others who can and will give you the truth in love and who are able to encourage you as you face obstacles and overcome challenges.

In every single thing that you do, remember that the choice is yours! Choose life, and give your time and attention to those things that will bring you peace, happiness, and hope. Faith comes by hearing, and so does fear—so be mindful of what you're exposing yourself and your family/friends to. I am so proud of my parents for choosing life and for realizing that they had children who loved them and wanted them to be whole. They chose to go to rehab and give their lives to the Lord and no one could've forced them to do that. Elizabeth A. Adams and John W. Dreher, I'm so proud to be called your daughter!

Always remember that the choice is yours!

Made in the USA
Columbia, SC
18 December 2018